EPSOM

THE TWENTIETH CENTURY

BRITAIN
IN OLD PHOTOGRAPHS

EPSOM

THE TWENTIETH CENTURY

PATRICIA BERRY

Sutton Publishing Limited
Phoenix Mill · Thrupp · Stroud
Gloucestershire · GL5 2BU

First published 2002

Copyright © Patricia Berry, 2002

Title page photograph: Grandstand, 1927.

British Library Cataloguing in Publication Data
A catalogue record for this book is available from the
British Library.

ISBN 0-7509-2770-4

Typeset in 10.5/13.5 Photina.
Typesetting and origination by
Sutton Publishing Limited.
Printed and bound in England by
J.H. Haynes & Co. Ltd, Sparkford.

CONTENTS

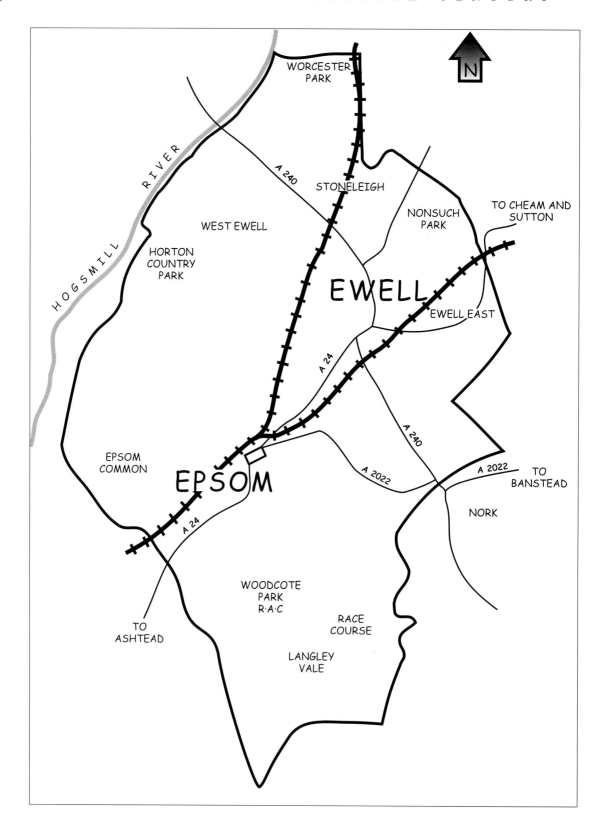

INTRODUCTION

'A mine of memories'

(*Aylmer's Field*, Tennyson)

An aged king's whim, a thirsty cow, some sporting gentlemen and the advent of the railway all helped create the Epsom of the dawn of the twentieth century. The small town, comprising several ancient settlements including Ebesham, Woodcote, Horton and Stamford, owed its Tudor prosperity to the visitors who came to view the splendours of Henry VIII's Nonsuch Palace, built over the remains of nearby Cuddington village. Within one hundred and fifty years the palace was dismantled, and it was not until 1959 that an archaeological dig revealed the extent and complexity of that wonder of its age, beloved by Henry and his daughter Elizabeth but misprized by later owners. Several old houses in Epsom incorporate building materials that may well have come from the debris of the palace.

A drought in the summer of 1618 brought about Epsom's next bout of prosperity when, so one story goes, a cowman named Wicker, who was trying to eke out a living on the Common, found a spring of water from which his cattle would not drink. It was subsequently discovered that although the water was unpleasant to the taste, applied externally it cleared up skin complaints, and those that ventured to slake their thirst with it were surprised at its purgative powers! Experts tell us it was the high content of magnesium sulphate that produced these effects. Whatever the reason, news of the latest wonder cure for all ills soon spread, wells were opened and Epsom became a spa, the fashionable place for the gentry to visit and take the waters. Visitors were closely followed by such entrepreneurs as were necessary to create a social centre, set in unspoilt countryside, yet a mere four-hour coach drive from London. And with the preparation and packaging of the local water in crystal form, the town's name passed into the English language, on its labelling as Epsom Salts.

It is sad that so little now remains to remind us of those heady times or to help us visualise what went on. Some idea of Epsom's importance in those early days can be gained from the fact that it was the first place outside the capital to have its own daily postal service.

Almost as quickly as it had arisen, the spa's popularity declined. Less efficient local wells were opened up, the originals put out of business and other spas such as Bath became the rage. The inns and lodging houses, shops and coffee rooms, bowling greens and theatres established to accommodate visitors were no longer patronised, though coaches plying between London and the south coast still came through and the very fine air and rural aspect encouraged members of the gentry to acquire country seats in the area. Epsom settled into a quiet market town with more than four hundred homes.

The town centre as seen from the Spread Eagle hotel, 1704, with pond and lock-up.

Away from today's busy main streets some attractive old mansions and smaller dwellings from this early period of prosperity can still be found, but in the town centre only the Albion, the Magpie, the Nell Gwynn, the Spread Eagle and Waterloo House (then the first assembly rooms in Europe, it is claimed) survive as silent witnesses to what had been. Of the elm, lime and yew trees that lined the streets leading to the wells, few remain, and it is hard to imagine the likes of Samuel Pepys and his friends strolling about the place, as they did of old.

As well as cock-fighting, prize-fighting and hawking, one of the pursuits indulged in during leisure hours spent away from the wells had been horse-racing. In the eighteenth century this was a cruel, arduous activity: the horses, usually at least five years old, ran several heats in one day over courses each of four miles or more. But from this activity grew the idea of shorter contests for younger horses, and, in 1779, Epsom saw its first of a new kind of race for three-year-old fillies who ran once round a one-and-a-half-mile course; it was called The Oaks, after the house nearby where the rules were formulated by a group of aristocratic sporting men. The next year, a similar race over one mile was introduced for three-year-old colts (and fillies), and this was named after Lord Derby, one of its instigators. Thus we come to the great resurgence of Epsom. In no time at all thousands were flocking to the Downs to join in the annual fun and excitement of that most famous of race meetings, so giving another local word to the English language.

Extraordinary sums of money were won and lost in wagers. Patronised by royalty, before long the Derby meeting became a highlight of the London season and Epsom's prosperity was assured. For some years the course – whose route was varied several times between 1780 and 1872 – was marked only by 'course-keepers' employed to clear the way between those standing spectators who might impede the horses' progress. At the time of suffragette Emily Davison's collision with the King's horse in 1913 (see p. 57), a simple post and rail was all that separated the crowds from the course, which was not completely fenced until 1929, I believe.

The first grandstand was built in 1830, to accommodate 5,000 under cover and a further 2,500 on the roof; it appears in the background of W.P. Frith's famous 1858 painting of a colourful cross-section of a Derby Day multitude. Extended in 1886 and 1900, it was not only a vantage point for visitors but behind the scenes were lock-ups, a small police court, and a printing room for last-minute production of race cards. In its early days it also housed the Clerk of the Course and his family.

The opening of the railway in 1847 brought not only increased trade and more inhabitants to the town, it meant that horses could be transported from other parts of the country to race; hitherto they had only managed to travel short distances by cart or on the hoof.

In the same year re-building began that would give Epsom the appearance it was to maintain for more than a century. The old watch-house by the pond in the centre of town, store for so long of the fire engine and headquarters of the constabulary, was replaced by the grand clock tower that still stands inimicably in the High Street. Soon the pond itself, deemed an insanitary eyesore by the nine members of the newly formed Local Board of Health, was filled in; impressive terraces of shops arose along the route to the railway station and elsewhere. Some twenty years later, the common fields were enclosed, estates broken up and housing developments began to infill previously open spaces. In 1899, just outside the time-span of this book, the Manor Hospital, first of Epsom's five mental asylums accommodating London County Council patients, opened on the old Horton estate; Horton, St Ebba's, Long Grove and West Park Hospitals would all follow before 1924. The staff required for the eventual eight thousand-plus inmates greatly increased Epsom's population.

When our story of the twentieth century begins, Epsom had been an Urban District for only six years; the Surrey Review Order of 1933 would expand the district to include parts

The winning post: artist's impression for the 'Owl' series of postcards.

of Cuddington, Ewell, Cheam and other neighbours. On Epsom's Charter Day (see pp. 106–8), 263 acres of Nonsuch Park (including The Mansion, developed from outbuildings of King Henry's palace) were dedicated for the joint use of the people of the boroughs of Epsom and Ewell, Sutton and Cheam. Later boundary changes have resulted in an area extending from Worcester Park in the north to Headley in the south, from Chessington in the west to Nork in the east, with a population at 1 January 2000 of 71,701.

The majority of illustrations that follow are from my own collection so they do not cover every aspect of the twentieth century in Epsom, and I apologise for any glaring omissions. For my first thirty years I lived at various addresses all within three miles of the town, which I came to know well. Throughout the Second World War I attended Nonsuch County School for Girls (see p. 90) and in the 1950s was fortunate enough to be employed in and around the town centre when many venerable buildings were still standing as reminders of an historic past. It was therefore a privilege to be asked to compile this book, to share my pride and pleasure in the town, to offer anecdotes and personal experiences, while showing the many changes that have come about and the many people who have been involved. It was a shock to realise that my life has covered almost three-quarters of the century under discussion, running parallel with radically altering social and political attitudes, from death in the workhouse and the unemployed roaming the countryside, through a world war (the second in the century) to the letting go of standards of behaviour, morals, and even dress.

Epsom's first police force: by 1912 it had increased sevenfold.

The Farm, Worcester Park. Agriculture was the main occupation of the area until the coming of the railway and rapid housing development.

Badge of the Urban District Council 1894–1937, with a representation of Nonsuch Palace.

ACKNOWLEDGEMENTS & BIBLIOGRAPHY

Iwould like to thank the following for their help and support in my preparation of this book: Shirley Murray, Christine Riley, Jean Taylor, Ron Stewart, Revd and Mrs Thomas, Rob Mann, Ken Harman, Joan Lea, Peter Sage, Carol Weston and the staffs of the Fawcett Society, Lester Bowden (Epsom), Seaford Library and Seaford Lighting; also Simon Fletcher, Joyce Percival, Michelle Tilling and Elizabeth Stone of Sutton Publishing Limited for editing, encouragement and understanding, and – last but never least – my old schoolfriends Audrey Seeley and Hilda Bristow (née Byles).

Illustrations marked * are reproduced by kind permission of the Croydon Advertiser Group. Those marked † appeared in the January 1951 edition of *Racing Review* which, in spite of every effort, I have been unable to trace. The current practice of marketing photographic copies of postcards and other illustrations means the original details of copyright, etc. are not available; apologies are rendered for any source not fully cleared or acknowledged, and a note to the publishers in such a case will ensure an amendment in any reprint.

Where my memory has failed or facts were otherwise unknown, I referred to the following:

Michael Wynn Jones, *The Derby* (Croom Helm Ltd, 1979).

Derby 200 official souvenir (*The Illustrated London News*, 1979).

John Casson, *Lewis and Sybil* (Collins, 1972).

Stuart Hibberd, *This . . . is London* (Macdonald & Evans, 1950).

Trevor White, *Epsom entertained!* (1989).

Stewart Granger, *Sparks fly upward* (London Granada, 1981).

David Rymill, *Worcester Park and Cuddington: a walk through the centuries* (Buckwheat Press, 2000).

John Sleight, *One-way Ticket to Epsom* (Bridge Studios, 1988).

A History of Ashtead (Leatherhead & District Local History Society, 1995).

1

The Town Centre

The Post Office, High Street. By 1897 the population of Epsom had risen to some 10,000, and new premises were needed for postal transactions. Small shops and cottages adjacent to the old Wellington Hotel were demolished and the neo-Tudor post office rose on the site (in use as such to this day). Schedules show that a number of the town's wall boxes had six collections a day, and the earliest time for the last collection was 7 p.m. There were four deliveries a day, the last at 6.40 p.m. In 1915 Miss Wallis and Miss Pott were employed on postal deliveries to relieve a man for army service in the First World War.

Tailoring

ALWAYS
UP-TO-DATE

Newest materials. Specially selected.
Best work by Experienced Hands.

J. Harvey,

HIGH STREET : EPSOM.

J. H. has always on hand a
large and well assorted stock
of

Boys' &
Youths'
Clothing

READY TO WEAR.

Best Value.
Latest Styles.

A TRIAL SOLICITED

The Spread Eagle crossroads, 1902. When the hotel (above) was built for Henry North in the early eighteenth century, its full title was the Black Spread Eagle. The traditional reason for the name is that such a bird formed part of the coat of arms of the Habsburg dynasty, from whose Rhineland vineyards North's best wines came. Through thick and thin the hotel has remained on the eastern corner of Ashley Road (see pp. 15 and 32); visible on its left here are Roll & Taylor's offices (formerly G. Nye) while far left are the business premises of Andrew's, printer and stationer (later Pullinger's) and beyond, part of the shop sign for Harvey's (1910 advertisement left).

High Street, 1905. Seemingly a very ordinary day in the High Street, but close inspection will reveal a number of points of interest; on the left, Sheath's Bakery, on the extreme right, the inn sign of the quaint old Shades pub with some fine exterior lanterns; to its left, the King's Head dating from the late seventeenth century, at this time proclaiming itself a commercial hotel, with its own pair of lampposts, and its neighbour known as the Nell Gwynn which has survived – amid the mayhem of redevelopment – into the twenty-first century.

Ashley Road, 1910. At right angles to the Spread Eagle inn were the single-storey premises of W. Bristow (see p. 17). The tall building with glass roof immediately beyond was a photographer's studio. This was the site for Reid's department store (see p. 27). In former times on racedays the forecourt of the Spread Eagle was a popular boarding-point for coaches up to the course at one shilling per person: hence the local cry 'A bob a nob'. Sir F. Standish's *Spread Eagle* was the 5–2 Derby winner in 1795.

Telephone P.O. 263.

C. Wells, draper. Mr Wells advertised himself as 'Linen draper, silk mercer, hosier and glover'. His premises in the High Street had showrooms for millinery, mantles and jackets, and his proposed expansion into 'Brighton House' was intended to cater for ladies' and children's outfitting and baby linen.

Elphick, butcher and grazier, 1910. Ardern Elphick traded at Aberdeen House, 2 West Street, adjacent to the forecourt of the Marquis of Granby public house, with a slaughter-house at the rear. Specialities included 'pickled tongues, calves' sweetbreads, home-killed and Scotch beef, Southdown and Scotch mutton, small dairy-fed pork'. It is only since the 1980s that the shop has changed its line of business.

Patronised by
His late
Majesty King
Edward VII
(when Prince
of Wales).

GARAGE. ALL REPAIRS.
INSPECTION PIT.

W. BRISTOW,

"Spread Eagle" Livery Stables,
HIGH STREET, EPSOM.

LANDAUS, BROUGHAMS and VICTORIAS

PONY-CARTS, PRIVATE BUSES & BRAKES
OF EVERY DESCRIPTION BY THE HOUR
OR JOB.

WEDDING & OTHER PARTIES
ATTENDED.

Telephones: 15 & 16 Epsom.

W. Bristow, livery stables. This advertisement from a guidebook of 1910 speaks for itself. In a town with more than the usual population of horses, craftsmen and traders with equine associations flourished at this time. Among the farriers, William Bristow had a forge at Waterloo House (see p. 29), and Churchill's in the narrow part of the High Street ('also at Ewell') supplied saddlery, harness, rugs, and a vast assortment of items essential to the owners of horses and carriages. In Upper High Street, Arthur Bowden founded the tailoring business which survives to this day (see p. 32), specialising in riding and racing wear.

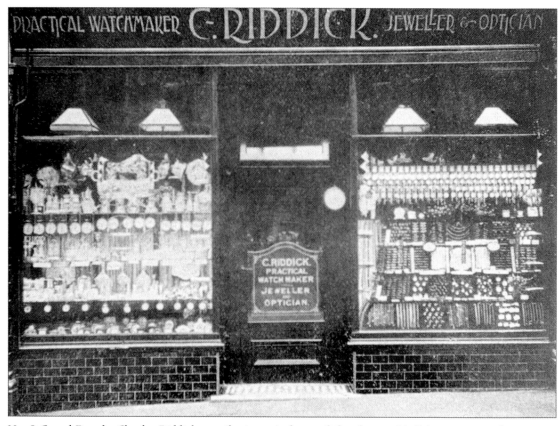

No. 9 Grand Parade. Charles Riddick was the tenant of one of the shops with living accommodation over in the Edwardian parade in Station Road (or Upper High Street). J. Sainsbury's (butchers, grocers and general provisions) came to Epsom to occupy another of these shops, until the early 1980s. In his 1910 advertisement Mr Riddick described himself as a practical watchmaker, jeweller and optician, undertaking contract clock-winding, repair and maintenance of barometers, and restoration and repair of electro- and silver-plated items.

Mittendorff House, 18 East Street, 1905. Dr Thomas John Barnardo established homes around the country 'for the protection, education and advancement of destitute children'. This house was named after its benefactor, Miss Mittendorff, and stood behind a high brick wall near the corner of Hook Road. Opposite was the twin-towered Electric Theatre, Epsom's first picture-house (silent), which opened in 1910 and to which sometimes all one hundred little boys over the road were invited for a special show. The home continued to shelter youngsters (who attended Pound Lane school) until the outbreak of the Second World War when all were evacuated, and the building was subsequently demolished. The cinema closed in the early 1920s and re-opened in 1926 as the Pavilion Theatre. Those who eagerly anticipated its re-opening after closing again 'for redecoration' in August 1929 were still waiting twenty-four years later when it was demolished. I can just about remember it, but only learned of its past glories from Mr Trevor White, that devoted recorder of the town's old entertainment centres.

Opposite: Ye Olde House, 115 High Street. Mr Riddington, who also traded in Sutton, acquired these premises in 1911 from the family firm of Barnard, who had catered for suppers, wedding breakfasts and other social occasions for over sixty years. I remember the diamond-paned windows of the tearoom (right), whose light was little help as you tumbled down the ancient step, just inside the door. This venerable building was an early victim of town-centre developers, being demolished in 1964 to make way for a National Westminster Bank.

East end of High Street, 1913. Sent as a Christmas card, this postcard view shows the narrow end of the High Street, with Church Street leading off left, and East Street to the right. The lamp standard bearing 'winged' signs directed traffic to Reigate (left) and London (right); in front of it stood the stone horse-troughs which on racedays served as wash-basins for visitors who had slept rough overnight. The first three-storey shop on the left was Mr Nuthall's grocery, the two-storey shop with white fascia-board was Daniell's newsagents and to the right of that (sun-blind out), the Epsom Meat Supply Company. The tall central building with four large lanterns was the Railway Inn. At one time the proprietor of the garage (far right) was Mr Richmond, whose charabanc and horsebox hire business later moved to South Street (see p. 25).

W.R. Page, 1910. From workshops in Waterloo Road, Page's expanded into showrooms in the High Street, next door to the post office. To coincide with the 1935 Silver Jubilee celebrations of King George V and Queen Mary, advertisements proudly stated that the firm had been 'established in Epsom during the reign of King Edward VII'. Two years later they suggested 'Why not buy a new car to celebrate Coronation Year?' – that of King George VI and Queen Elizabeth.

Opposite: Station Road (Upper High Street). Rightly named in the 1920s, it then led to the old Epsom Town/Croydon line railway station, established in 1847. On the corner site, occupied here by Chilton & Paine drapers (later Coppens), formerly stood Ormonde House, home and business premises of Mr Henry Dorling and his large family. His step-daughter Isabella, after marriage to Sam Beeton, became famous for her *Book of Household Management* and other compendiums of advice for women. *Ormonde* was the 1886 Derby winner, ridden by the legendary jockey Fred Archer. What a combination! Archer rode five Derby winners and Ormonde won every race in which he was entered.

High Street, looking east. Dated 1924–5, this view of the town centre shows War Pensions Committee rooms on the left, still needed six years after the Armistice ended the First World War. The post office was next door. Beyond the crossroads, one can get some idea of how narrow that part of High Street was. The story goes that it was the displeasure of King George V at being caught there in a traffic jam en route to the Derby that brought about road widening in 1934–5. Near the camera far right is Riddington's cake shop and tea-room (p. 18), as I remember it up to the 1950s; next door, Lester Bowden's outfitters (see p. 32) – once Hoffman's music warehouse, and, at the time of writing, Waterstone's bookshop.

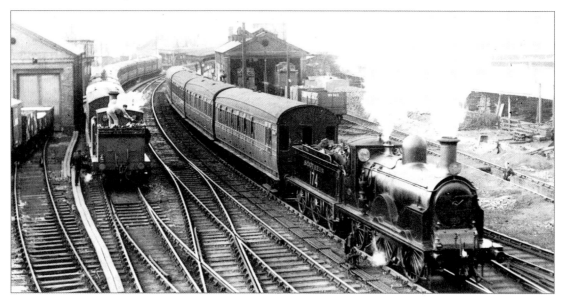

Epsom Town station, 1927–8. Epsom's first trains arrived at this station when the London, Brighton & South Coast Railway extended the line from Croydon in 1847. Twelve years later it was linked to Leatherhead, and continued in existence, with the rival London & South Western railway line via Wimbledon on the other side of town from 1859. On Saturday 2 February 1901 the funeral train conveying the body of Queen Victoria, attended by chief mourner King Edward VII, 'His Imperial Majesty the German Emperor and the other royal princes' passed through Epsom. The old station was in use for little more than a year after this photograph was taken: in 1929 a new station was built off Waterloo Road and from then on both lines ran into it.

Point duty, High Street/Ashley Road/Waterloo Road. Before traffic-lights were installed at this busy crossroads, police control was essential. It always fascinated me to watch a constable arrive at the scene, draw on his long white cuffs and step confidently in among the vehicles. In later years, when a royal motorcade came down from the racecourse, all lights at this spot were set at red or off and a constable stood on each corner to safeguard the onlookers crowding the pavements as they waited for a glimpse of the cars and their occupants.

The Clock Tower and north side of High Street, February 1930. 'H.C.T.', the subject of this snapshot, was obliging enough to date it. Seven-and-a-half years later, on 29 September 1937, hundreds of citizens gathered in the area to witness the formal presentation of the charter granting Epsom and Ewell borough status. Here, cars are parked where once was the large pond, condemned and drained by the local Health Board in 1854, at the same time that the nearby watch house was demolished and the Clock Tower built (see Introduction).

New fire/ambulance station, Church Street. Epsom's early fire brigade had no headquarters as its equipment was housed in different parts of the town, but in 1911 a small station was built in Church Street. Coinciding with the granting of borough status (1937), a modern building (above) with living accommodation for the firemen was erected on the site. The Chief Officer at that time was Mr A.G. Page (left).

The Clock Tower, 1950s. This is the west end of the High Street, as older residents will remember it before the developers moved in. Buildings to the left of the girl cyclist include Page Motors (see p. 21) and the post office (see p. 13), with a partial view of the Spread Eagle Hotel behind the tower. For many years there were public conveniences in the basement of the Clock Tower; it housed an information centre in the 1990s. Buildings on the right of the picture include the Nell Gwynne tearooms and the seventeenth-century King's Head Hotel. Cars parked in the central area (except on market days) as did the mobile coffee bar: compare with 2001 (see p. 31).

Epsom Coaches. As business flourished, Mr H.R. Richmond moved his premises from High Street (see p. 20) to South Street. His son Roy joined the family firm after the Second World War, and saw it expand into bus services and holiday travel. I remember Roy from the 1950s when Richmond Coaches were hired to take the local baseball team, the Epsom Lions, to away matches (see p. 94).

Spread Eagle crossroads, 1959. Witnessed by one cyclist, four loungers and a woman shopper, the new bride waves to guests at the hotel wedding reception from the back of the honeymoon car, 'destination secret'. In fact it went only a few yards to the railway station where the young couple entrained for Bracklesham Bay. Background buildings include Longley & Broadhurst estate agents, the White Hart Hotel (inn sign only), the post office, the Wellington Inn and the Westminster Bank.

Waterloo Road. Half a century ago Dorset's ironmongers (established 1828) were trading not so far from their former premises at the crossroads of High Street and Waterloo Road. In 1906 the old buildings were demolished and rebuilt for Dorset's at Number 68 (with a 'trademark' plough on the roof) and the London & County (later Westminster) Bank next door on the corner. When traffic-light standards were installed at all four corners of the crossroads, the one outside the bank left little room on the pavement for pedestrians. Out of the picture, to the right, the building originally used as the Wesleyan Church later became the Foresters Hall. One frosty New Year's Eve in the 1950s, I was part of a forty-strong Conga line which wound its way through streets around the hall, as midnight struck. It was distressing in later years to watch the decline (and eventual fall) of a building with many such happy memories.

Reid's the Courtesy Store, 1959. 'The West End store in Epsom' with 'eighteen departments under one roof' was erected in the early 1930s, with lift, hairdressing salon and roof garden, on the site of Bristow's livery stables (see p. 17). H.L. Reid's was originally a draper's shop at Surrey House, High Street, where in 1910 it was claimed 'ladies can rely upon getting courteous attention'. The Ebbisham Hall (off to the right) opened in the autumn of 1929 and was licensed for use for a variety of musical and other events.

High Street looking west, 1970s. In 1938, a scheme was begun to widen this part of the High Street to 75 ft, demolish the old properties, set back the north pavement and develop new shops. Building was suspended during the Second World War, with further delays caused by post-war restrictions and shortages. Eventually, by the early 1950s the long parade of shops in neo-Georgian style was completed; a number of chain stores moved in, with few local traders represented. Five units in from the right (with fan decoration above first-floor windows) in lieu of the old Railway Inn was the Charter Inn, later broken up into separate establishments. Shops far left survived much longer.

The Ashley Centre. From the mid-1950s the historic High Street buildings began to disappear, replaced by modern substitutes of little character. The culmination of this redevelopment was the creation of the vast Ashley Centre, with branches of many leading stores and a multi-storey car park. Officially opened by Her Majesty the Queen on 24 October 1984, the centre, now including offices and the Epsom Playhouse (see p. 30), occupies much of the area bounded by High Street, Ashley Road, Ashley Avenue and South Street.

High Street/South Street/West Street, *c.* 1992. Until 1971 this site of Sainsbury's store (above) was occupied by Epsom's Odeon cinema. Seating more than 1,400 patrons, it was one of thirty-six in Oscar Deutsch's countrywide chain to be built in 1937. After its demolition a decade passed before the supermarket was erected.

Far right (below) is another view with a reminder of Epsom's heady days as a spa. Built in the 1690s as the New Tavern (later Waterloo House), it was the last word in design and amenities, featuring a central arcade flanked by fashionable shops and with carriage access from the road, so that passengers could alight under cover. A tall arched window still to be seen in the west side wall is a relic of one original entrance door. Long rooms with views of a bowling green were available for dancing and gaming, while upstairs, overlooking the comings and goings in the High Street, were coffee rooms and the tavern. With the decline of the wells some seventy years on, the New Tavern shops fell from favour and closed down. From late Victorian times a succession of drapers occupied all or part of the building – Oldridge, Bailey, Wheeler Brothers and (by the 1950s) Ely's.

The Playhouse, Ashley Avenue. One especially happy outcome of the redevelopment of the High Street/Ashley Road/South Street area as the Ashley Centre (see p. 28) was the creation of this theatre, opened in 1983. Seating four hundred, it has been the setting for many theatrical productions, concerts, movie shows and the like. It incorporates the smaller Myers Hall, which was built to seat eighty, plus attractive refreshment areas, open daily, and exhibition space.

Ashley Road. A lone tree marks the site of P.C. King's carefully tended garden in front of the 'bungalow' police station; the upper storey had been destroyed by enemy action in the Second World War. This was the building raided in 1919 by Canadian troops from Woodcote Park convalescent camp (see p. 105) in an attempt to release two comrades arrested for disorderly behaviour. In the struggle that ensued, Station Sergeant Green was killed. On re-siting Ashley Avenue as part of the new ring road system – the route of the original avenue now followed by a ramp from the Ashley Centre car park – the police station was demolished and modern premises opened in Church Street.

Near the Clock Tower. A one-way traffic system and some pedestrianising in 1991, followed two years later by the official opening of the Market Place (up-holding rights granted in 1685), have created safe sites for stalls and browsers. This photograph was taken on a Monday, with few customers about. It is interesting to see a refreshment van still playing a vital part in the market community (see p. 25). Far left in the distance is the Albion, once a coffee house and part of John Levingstone's attempt in 1707 to rival the original wells on the Common, by setting up the New Wells complete with shops, gardens and bowling green. I have been told that at one time the Albion's front room upstairs served as the magistrate's court.

Meeting House, Prospect Place. At first glance an area completely rebuilt as sheltered units, this backstreet still offers an important reminder of times long past. Today in use as offices, this building was erected in the 1770s as a chapel for early nonconformists. In my five years' exploration of Epsom half a century ago, I was never aware of the chapel or of the old cottages that then surrounded it.

Lester Bowden at the Spread Eagle. From a tailor's shop in Upper High Street founded by his father Arthur, Lester Bowden moved in 1927 to the former music store at 109–113 High Street (see p. 22). For more than sixty years the family traded there as suppliers of riding clothes and equipment with a clientele that included royalty. The fine old building with its oak staircases and panelled walls, once displaying racing mementoes, silks, trophies and saddlery, has now passed into other hands, but the similar interior of the old coaching inn makes an excellent alternative setting.

Derby Square. A complex of shops, apartments, piazzas and a public library (opened May 2001), Derby and Oaks Squares were developed on land for some years used as a car park and open space between the rear of High Street and the Victoria line railway embankment. Some buildings sport mosaic motifs, following through the racing theme.

2
Ewell (with Stoneleigh & Worcester Park)

Christian Endeavour group. 'A walk near Ewell' is the only clue to the location of this charming sepia photograph, rescued in two pieces from an old album. The walkers include members of the Brown and Fea families.

Class II, Ewell Girls' School, *c.* 1903. In 1861, on land given by Sir George Glyn, the National School opened in West Street. It catered for boys aged seven to fourteen years, girls in the same age group, and mixed infants five to seven years old. These girls would have had to climb an external staircase to reach their first floor classrooms. In 1913 girls and infants moved into a new building alongside the old, which closed in 1971, when modern premises were built in Longmead Road.

The Long Spring. This view looks north towards the spot where the High Street was extended in 1834 to link London Road with the village. Until then the only route was by way of Church Street with a hazardous right-angled bend where fatal accidents had been known to happen. The Spring Hotel (see p. 36) is in the middle distance and, far right, the boundary wall and trees of Rectory House, home of the Glyn family (see p. 39). The postcard from which this scene was taken was sent on 28 July 1907 by a young woman employed locally at 'Shalimar', evidently at that time a large establishment, as she mentions 'five maids kept, three men and a boy outside'.

Lower Mill. The message with this beautifully tinted postcard issued by Ewell stationers, Brunton and Williams, was written by someone convalescing in Epsom and enjoying 'the gardens, the fine trees and flowers, the song of blackbirds and thrushes'. This mill had been on Chertsey Abbey land; at one time it was involved in the making of paper. The year before the Second World War began, a serious fire destroyed the mill but the eighteenth-century house survived.

The Packhorse Bridge. By the mid-eighteenth century a forty-five-acre site near Ewell Court (see p. 39) was given over to an enterprise on the Hogsmill for the production of gunpowder. At its height more than 150 people were working there. Explosions were frequent, sometimes with fatalities (at least three graves in St Mary's churchyard) and eventually local magistrates refused to renew the necessary licences. The mill closed in 1875 and all traces of it have been obliterated. But the nearby packhorse bridge has survived (several times restored) and is now an attractive feature of the local recreation grounds. Such bridges were built without side walls or parapets so that, no matter the width of their loads, horses and mules could cross unhindered.

High Street, looking north. The woman who sent this postcard view to her little boy Eric, at home in Kent in 1906, had just won four coconuts at Epsom racecourse fair, but failed to back any winners. All buildings featured still stand ninety-five years later, though some are used for very different purposes.

The horse pond, 1909. This large pond follows the curve of Chessington Road as it joins the junction of Kingston Road and London Road (as cut through in 1834 to relieve traffic hazards in the village). The Spring Hotel, behind fence and bushes on the left, was once a farmhouse; the wall to the right is the boundary of Garbrand Hall (see p. 38). The soothing waters of the pond were welcome not only to the horses: the iron rims of cartwheels needed to be cooled off too.

The High Street. Looking south towards Bank Corner – to the left of the horse-drawn cart, and below – this postcard view was another produced by stationers Brunton and Williams. The right-hand tree marks the approximate position of their shop. With the King William IV public house opposite, it is not surprising that the area was once known locally as Williams' Corner – not so with the pub's earlier name of the George and Dragon. Near left are the timber-framed buildings with protruding upper storeys dating from Tudor times.

Bank Corner. The London Provincial Bank occupied this ancient building on the blind corner of Cheam Road and High Street, with the nineteenth-century Star Inn, a Charrington house, far left in this postcard view. Far right is the Congregational chapel built in 1865, one of its sponsors being Mr J.C. Sharpe of the gunpowder mills (see p. 35). A founder member was 76-year-old Miss Mary Wallis, a remarkable lady who from her wage as a domestic servant (from the age of nine) had in twenty-seven years saved a sufficient sum to have a tiny wooden chapel built in 1825 for local non-conformists.

Garbrand Hall (Bourne Hall). The gateway was one of the additions made to the hall (built in about 1770 as the country seat of a London wine merchant) when acquired some twenty-five years later by Mr T.H. Barritt. The hound (talbot) on top was part of his coat of arms; it lost its original tail (an eyewitness says) in a heavy air raid in the Second World War. The estate changed hands several times until by the 1880s Mrs George Torr's fifteen-acre grounds were famous for the wide range of plants and trees growing there. In 1925 its name was changed to Bourne Hall and housed a girls' school with a strict notice at the gate: 'For the daughters of professional gentlemen'. The school colours were light blue and maroon with the hound incorporated in the badge. Bourne Hall School closed without prior notice after the summer holidays of 1953; the building stood empty and deteriorated for nine years until later it was demolished. (see p. 49.)

Sir Arthur R. Glyn Bart, JP, CA. Most of the older people who gave me their recollections of Ewell included a 'snapshot' of Sir Arthur 'striding by, walking to his committees in Kingston', or some similar description. Descendant of two eighteenth-century Lord Mayors of London (one of them a founder of Glyn Mills Bank), and of a nineteenth-century Vicar of Ewell, he became the seventh Baronet Glyn in 1921. He entered wholeheartedly into the life of the village, supporting many of its societies and athletic clubs: he was President of Ewell Old Boys' Association, for example. At Epsom's charter celebrations on 29 September 1937, as Second Substitute Charter Mayor he rode in the fifth coach immediately behind the mayor's state coach, with First Substitute Charter Mayor Councillor J.S. Underhill and Mrs Underhill.

Ewell Court, 1937. Built for Mr J.H. Bridges, former proprietor of the gunpowder mills (see p. 35) in 1879, the house was acquired by the district authority in 1935. It was used as a local Food Office in the years of rationing during and after the Second World War, and has gone on serving the community in different capacities.

St Francis's Parish Church, 1939. The church, on the corner of Ruxley Lane and Scotts Farm Road, was consecrated by the Bishop of Guildford on 25 May 1939. Less than sixty years later, subsidence caused the building to be declared unsafe. The congregation last worshipped here on 9 February 1997, after which demolition took place. Services have since been held jointly with the nearby Methodist church.

The Horse Pond, 1949. Forty years on from our last look at the pond (see p. 36), small boys instead of horses find this a cool spot on a bright summer's day. The Spring Hotel (left) has become bolder in advertising itself, and traffic lights have been installed at the crossroads in the distance.

Lansdowne College. Close to the most northerly point of the borough today, the College stood in The Avenue (earlier known as the Grand or Great Avenue). It was a girls' school founded in the late 1860s by three sisters, the Misses J. and E. Turk and Mrs F. Carter. Prior to demolition in the mid-1930s, the house had been used as an hotel. Lansdowne Court was developed on the site.

Royal Avenue, looking south. Following a line roughly north–south, this may have been the sovereign's route from Hampton Court to Nonsuch Palace (see Introduction). The view is towards St Mary's Road and the site of Worcester House in the Great Park, built as Keeper's Lodge for Edward Somerset, fourth Earl of Worcester. When Samuel Pepys was at Nonsuch on behalf of the Navy Office, he sometimes dined at Worcester House with a later occupant, Sir Robert Long, who achieved high office under King Charles II.

St Clement's Catholic Church, 1956. Though Father F.E. Young had been in Ewell only since 1952, he was celebrating twenty-five years in the priesthood at the reception arranged by his parishioners at the Stoneleigh Hotel. A parochial committee chaired by Mr W.T. Hughes had organised a collection amounting to two hundred guineas (£210). The presentation was made by Mr J. Moore (right). *

Round Table Fête, 1956. Ewell and Worcester Park Round Table organised a fête and fairground on 2 June at The Green, Worcester Park, to raise money for local charities. The sum of about £130 was realised. *

Worcester Park House. The house dated from about 1797, with later improvements under the direction of John Nash, the architect of London's Regent Street. Various well-to-do families lived in the house from Victorian times until just before the outbreak of the Second World War. A fire brought about the end of a once elegant mansion, leaving open land between Grafton Road and Old Malden Lane.

The Light of the World, 1854. Two leading members of the Pre-Raphaelite Brotherhood of painters had links with the area of the Hogsmill and surrounding countryside. John Millais often stayed with the Lemprière family at Worcester Park Farm; his *Ophelia in the Stream* and *A Huguenot on St Bartholomew's Eve* both have local settings. William Holman Hunt, nephew of William Hobman of Rectory Farm, Ewell, painted his *Hireling Shepherd* near Ewell Court Farm, and chose part of an abandoned hut in the grounds of the old powdermill for the door in his portrayal of Christ: 'Behold, I stand at the door and knock'. From June to November they worked out of doors, Holman Hunt often painting through the night by moon- and lantern-light, sheltering in a bivouac of shepherd's hurdles. The design of the east window in Ewell Parish Church was inspired by the painting, a copy of which, hanging at the west end of the church, miraculously escaped when fire in 1973 caused major damage to the lady chapel, organ and north aisle.

The Broadway, Stoneleigh, 1930s. When Nonsuch Palace was demolished, its lands were given over for agricultural use. The major farms were called Bowling Green, Sparrow, Coldharbour and Worcester Park. In 1860 the first-named became the property of Mr J.J. Stone, hence came the title Stoneleigh. Mr Stone willed that his trustees should hold fire on selling the land at farming rates, awaiting the day when housing development plans would put up prices. This took over fifty years. The new estate was promoted at an Ideal Homes Exhibition in the early 1930s, when at last house prices began to go up. Some of the first pupils at Nonsuch County School for Girls, which opened in May 1937, came from these new houses; their route home was across the park to Sparrow Farm Road. A resident of Stoneleigh Park Road at about this time was young John Osborne; in reminiscences of Nonsuch Park recorded after his success as a playwright he struck many a familiar chord with me but also stirred up memories long buried.

The Broadway, Stoneleigh, 1950s. With Dell Road off to the left of the roundabout and Woodside Avenue to the right, straight ahead is the south-east approach to the railway station, opened in July 1932 on the Waterloo to Epsom line in anticipation of the large numbers of Londoners who would be tempted to move to the Surrey countryside. For a while the station stood on open land but houses and shops soon began to appear. Builders Wimpey offered detached three-bedroom houses for less than £750, or 17s 6d per week rent.

Worcester Park orchestral concert, 1945. On Saturday mornings, player-pupils from Sutton County Boys' School, Nonsuch County School for Girls and elsewhere joined forces to rehearse music in the hall of Balmoral Road School, quite near St Philip's Church. Some of us were also linked with the senior orchestra; I served as a sort of back-up music librarian, page-turner and maid-of-all-work. The December concert included Beethoven's Egmont Overture and Schubert's Unfinished Symphony; the Wesley Hall in which it was held had been opened in October 1938, after years of planning and fund-raising by local Methodists, their different factions having been successfully re-united six years before.

By coincidence, they were to be called on to make a second change of direction when with the approval of the Bishop of Southwark, ecumenically integrated services were adopted in late 1990 with the congregation of St Philip's, deemed dangerous through subsidence and later demolished (see St Francis's, p. 40).

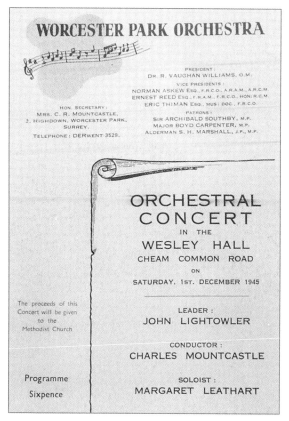

WORCESTER PARK ORCHESTRA

PRESIDENT :
DR. R. VAUGHAN WILLIAMS, O.M.

VICE PRESIDENTS :
NORMAN ASKEW ESQ., F.R.C.O., A.R.A.M., A.R.C.M.
ERNEST REED ESQ., F.R.A.M., F.R.C.O., HON: R.C.M.
ERIC THIMAN ESQ., MUS : DOC., F.R.C.O.

HON. SECRETARY :
MRS. C. R. MOUNTCASTLE,
2, HIGHDOWN, WORCESTER PARK,
SURREY.
TELEPHONE : DERWENT 3529.

PATRONS :
SIR ARCHIBALD SOUTHBY, M.P.
MAJOR BOYD CARPENTER, M.P.
ALDERMAN S. H. MARSHALL, J.P., M.P.

ORCHESTRAL CONCERT
IN THE
WESLEY HALL
CHEAM COMMON ROAD
ON
SATURDAY, 1ST. DECEMBER 1945

The proceeds of this Concert will be given to the Methodist Church

LEADER :
JOHN LIGHTOWLER

CONDUCTOR :
CHARLES MOUNTCASTLE

Programme
Sixpence

SOLOIST :
MARGARET LEATHART

Shadbolt Park. Mr Ernest I. Shadbolt, railway engineer and keen collector of rare trees and shrubs, came to live in Worcester Park on retirement. At the very northern extremity of today's Cuddington ward, Shadbolt House was built to his own ecology-conscious requirements, many far ahead of their time. On his death in 1936 the property was acquired by the Borough, and the gardens have been open to the public ever since.

The Dipping Place, High Street. The springs from which the Hogsmill river has its source – and which may well have encouraged first-century Romans to settle here – rose clear and vigorous in this area. The river was deep and strong enough to turn mill-wheels, and to be featured in John Everett Millais' famous painting of the drowning Ophelia (see p. 45). Improvements have come about through the landscaping of Bourne Hall grounds and general interest in conserving and enhancing the natural surroundings of the village.

War memorial, the Dipping Place. After the 1918 Armistice towns and villages throughout the country set about creating memorials to honour those who had died in the First World War. Eighty names were listed on the panel now located by the Long Spring. It was formerly fixed on the outer wall between the doors of the lock-up in Church Street. In the parish churchyard is a catafalque-style memorial in a paved area, for which a maintenance trust was initiated by Mr T. Martin.

Bourne Hall, Spring Street. Replacing the girls' school of the same name (see p. 38), this 'space-age' circular building opened in February 1970, incorporating a public library, large and small halls and a museum which features a collection of large industrial items from the past. The grounds and lake have been revitalised; in one corner of the gardens (below) I found squirrels, swans and statues, the last perhaps a survivor from Mrs Torr's fifteen acres, so celebrated in the late nineteenth century.

High Street/Cheam Road corner. Now extended to occupy the former London Provincial Bank premises (see p. 37), the Star Inn continues to flourish. The tree and lamp standard (above) mark the former site of the Congregational church, demolished in 1938 when a larger church (now United Reformed) opened in London Road. Mercifully the site has not been redeveloped with intrusive modernism; instead it presents a welcome patch of green, the Longhurst garden (left).

The Grove, 2001. Still an impressively rural link between two busy Ewell roads, High Street and West Street, this shady walk is believed to be more than three hundred years old. It was probably planted with lime trees to mark King William III's accession to the throne in 1689. After continuing south-east across the old Fair Field as part of Reigate Road, it meets the conjectured line of Roman Stane Street; I like to think that this route, near which Roman coins and other archaeological discoveries have been made, was in use almost two thousand years ago.

Bourne Hall garden, 2001. This illustrated sign in Bourne Hall's grounds near the lake features several local anecdotes – the Garbrand hound saving a child from drowning, the prisoner in the lock-up drinking smuggled ale through his clay pipe, swan-upping and roasting, and the 'flying saucer' design of the Hall, controversial in 1970. The sign is intended to encourage visitors to explore Sections 7 and 8 (Epsom and Ewell/Kingston upon Thames) of the London Loop, 150 miles of footpaths encircling the capital.

Ewell Watch House, 2001. Externally little changed since my childhood trips to the village (a short ride with mother on the 408 green bus from Cheam crossroads), this late eighteenth-century building served as lock-up and fire engine store. In spite of this curious juxtaposition, our visits to the spot were solemn, as mother explained that the writing between the doors was a list of poor soldiers from Ewell who had died in the First World War. (Limbless and shell-shocked survivors were often encountered in our streets, more than a decade after the Armistice.) This memorial has since been moved to the Dipping Place by the main entrance to Bourne Hall (see p. 48).

The Green Man, 2001. There has been an inn of this name (referring perhaps to a forester or woodman) on the site since the mid-eighteenth century, though the present building was erected in the 1930s, when there was a bus stop immediately outside. As a small child travelling on the 408 (as above), I always expected a Biblical character to jump on board: I misinterpreted the conductor's cry of 'Green Man Ewell' as 'Emmanuel'. A century ago the inn gave its name to the street, later known as High Street.

3

The Racecourse

Grandstand, 1904. Before writing, at 2 p.m. on 15 September 1904, to their friend Nell in Margate, Flo and her friend Ede had purchased this rare view-card from photographer Mr J.G. Tillett's shop in Church Street (see p. 104) and then ridden their bicycles up to the course. One hopes the weather had improved since the 'Thunderstorm Derby' earlier that year, when two spectators were struck by lightning. My grandparents, attempting to walk home via the Drift Bridge (see p. 68) were cut off by floods, and Gran made part of the journey slung over her husband's shoulder, as he waded waist-deep through the swirling water.

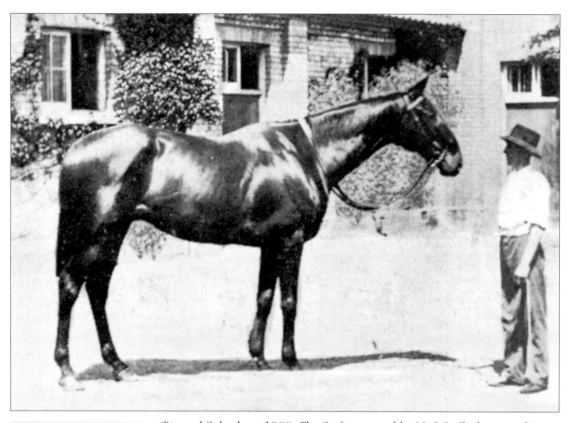

City and Suburban, 1900. *The Grafter*, owned by Mr J.G. Clarke, won this race and the Prince Edward Handicap in the same year. (From an Ogden's cigarette card.)

Lester Reiff, 1901. A 'Spy' caricature of the American champion jockey in 1900, who the following year won the Derby on *Volodyovski* at 5–2. Only a few months later he was warned off by the Jockey Club for aggressive riding and other unacceptable behaviour. His brother Johnny won the Derby in 1907 on *Orby*. Both winners were American-owned. The 1913 Derby, already blighted by the tragedy of suffragette Emily Davison's collision with the King's horse (see p. 57), was further marred by Johnny, on the favourite *Craganour*, bumping and boring the leader, 100–1 outsider *Aboyeur*, as they approached the finish. He was first past the post, but was disqualified in favour of *Aboyeur*.

On the road, Derby Day, Epsom, *c.* 1911. This magnificent evocation of an Edwardian race day comes from an undated, unposted 'genuine silver print photograph' postcard, the pride of my collection. It shows several elements of those special days, with the working man (far left) selling race cards and the trader in a straw hat stepping into the street for a moment to watch the traffic pass by. Then we have the smart mounted policeman and the folk making their way towards the Downs on foot, in flat-top carts, in elegant open carriages . . . and the horse-chestnut trees are in bloom.

The Durdans, 1905. F.A. Daniell, newsagent of 27 High Street, published this postcard thirty years after Archibald Philip Primrose, fifth Earl of Rosebery and the hope of the Liberal party, came to live here and develop an indoor riding school and stables in the grounds of his house. Nearby are buried equine racing giants such as the Derby winners *Amato* (1838, owner Sir Gilbert Heathcote), *Ladas* (1894), *Sir Visto* (1895) and *Cicero* (1905), all three owned by Lord Rosebery. Two or even three earlier houses stood on the site, one incorporating building materials from King Henry VIII's newly demolished Nonsuch Palace (see Introduction), another burnt to the ground before completion. Lord Rosebery was Gladstone's Foreign Secretary in 1886 and 1892, and Prime Minister from 1894 to 1895.

They're off! A faded photograph from someone's cherished album recalls the scene some ninety years ago, as the colourful mass of horses and riders begins its mile-and-a-half long journey to the winning post. Though the original start was much nearer Langley Bottom, by 1900 the Derby course had been established for twenty-eight years on the route it still takes today. There is a steep downward gradient (one in eighteen) over the first five hundred yards.

The Downs Hotel. In 1910, with his name in tall letters along the roofline, the proprietor was Mr E.J. Clarke. Twenty years later his son Nigel, a professional actor, founded Epsom Little Theatre at the Ebbisham Hall. Mr Clarke senior offered 'good rooms, cooking and attendance, stabling and garage' and dispensed the ales, stout and porter of R. & F. Pagden. Overlooking the paddock and winning post and with extensive views of the racecourse and Downs, the hotel later became a Friary Meux house.

Emily Wilding Davison BA (from a memorial card). Miss Davison died in Epsom Cottage Hospital on Sunday 8 June 1913 after a collision with King George V's horse *Anmer*, during the running of the Derby. With a First Class degree in English Language and Literature, she had been a teacher for thirteen years before becoming a full-time member of the militant WSPU, campaigning for full women's suffrage. Her aggressive work for the cause resulted in a number of fines and prison sentences. She and her colleagues were harshly regarded by government, public, police and prison authorities alike; they claimed the privileges of political prisoners but were treated as common criminals – their response was to stage hunger strikes. These came to be regularly countered by the horrors of forcible feeding. Emily suffered this outrage no fewer than forty-one times in the last four years of her life. One day, when doctor and wardresses had done their worst on her and moved on to her colleagues in neighbouring cells, she conceived a desperate plan to distract the group by throwing herself down an iron staircase, at least a thirty-foot drop: 'one big tragedy may save many others'. At a third attempt, to a cry of 'No surrender!' she was partially successful, injuring her head, neck, back and shoulders in a fall of some ten feet. Within forty-eight hours her forcible feeding was resumed. From a bright, attractive girl, Emily at forty was a battle-scarred veteran, her suffering showing in her face. One wonders if her mind had also been affected, resulting in her fatal dash on to the racecourse that awful day: her motives have never been satisfactorily explained. A road in the new Royal Drive estate at Tattenham Corner has recently been named Emily Davison Drive.

Racecourse and old grandstand. Still looking very much an all-male affair, the above postcard view of punters, bookies, layabouts and the temporary accommodation on the Hill suggests the continuing reliance on horse-drawn transport. As they look across to the finishing post (below) the number of boaters indicates a reasonably fine day: not so in three successive years 1924 to 1926, when heavy rain reduced the Derby course and surrounding downland to deep mud. My grandfather remembered seeing motor cars approaching the area loaded with straw bales as a precaution; other drivers who found their vehicles axle-deep in mud had to rely on local farmers with their tractors.

Derby winners. Jockey Steve Donaghue (see p. 62) had already ridden three Derby winners (*Pommern* 1915, *Guy Crusader* 1917 – both at Newmarket during the First World War – and *Humorist* 1921) when he steered Lord Woolavington's horse *Captain Cuttle* (above) to victory four lengths clear of the field in 1922. There had been last-minute drama in the paddock when *Captain Cuttle* seemed to go lame; then it was found he had shed a plate. Swift work by the course farrier, and with seconds to spare, 'our Steve' brought his mount to the start, but not before bookies, anticipating difficulties, lengthened the odds to 10–1. The following year Donaghue rode not for Lord Woolavington but for Mr B. Irish; *Papyrus* (right) trained by Basil Jarvis won by a length from *Pharos* at odds of 100–15. This illustration is taken from a Turf cigarette card published by Alexander Boguslavsky of Piccadilly, London W1.

The new stand, 1927. The six-month General Strike of 1926 almost put paid to the construction of the new grandstand (above) but, apart from lifts to the upper balconies, it was ready in time for the 1927 Derby. This was won by the 4–1 favourite *Call Boy* ridden by Charlie Elliott and owned by Mr Frank Curzon. Desperately ill, Mr Curzon was able to lead in his winner, but was dead a month later. Among distinguished visitors to the meeting was American aeronaut Colonel Charles Augustus Lindbergh (below) who only a few days earlier (Sunday 29 May) had landed at Croydon Airport from France, following his 33½-hour flight across the Atlantic in his *Spirit of St Louis*.

Charabancs, *c.* 1930. With open sun-roofs, these 'charras' allowed a grandstand view of the final straight. These undated snapshots neatly convey the atmosphere of a day out in the interwar years: (above) looking towards Tattenham Corner, (below) a view across to the Hill. The wide variations in female costume suggests the weather could not make up its mind, either.

Jockey Steve Donahue. As a lad, Steve walked to Chester from his home in Warrington and found work at stables in Kingsclere. Later, as a successful jockey, he won the Derby on six occasions (see p. 59). A tremendous favourite with the crowd, whose 'Come on, Steve' was for years a catchphrase to encourage slowcoaches, in use well beyond racing circles, he supported many local fund-raising activities. In 1933 he took part in the donkey derby arranged for the summer fête at St Anthony's Hospital, North Cheam, and won. It is said in my family that on that occasion (or a similar one), the great man shook me by the hand; as I was only two at the time, I have to rely on their memories.

Racecourse catchphrases. My father, a great sporting man, mimic and musician, attended as many Derby meetings as work would allow, walking from Belmont across the Downs to Epsom. Consequently family conversations in my childhood were peppered with phrases he had heard there, such as 'Come on, Steve', 'I gotta horse' (tipster Ras Prince Monolulu, see p. 63), 'Bob a nob' (see p. 15), 'You've got a lucky face, dear' (gypsy fortune-tellers) and – my favourite – 'Joe Assenheim's at two' (right). This was the call of the ice-cream seller, meaning tuppence a time.

Regular raceday features. Bizarre and colourful characters made their way to Epsom for the Derby and other meetings; there was plenty for visitors to see and do between races. There were gypsies in their immaculate caravans, sandwich-board men with signs announcing that the end of the world was nigh, entertainers and stunt-men like the escapologist (above), religious mission meetings – with voices raised in hymn-singing to vie with the bookies' cries, and tipsters in eye-catching costumes, often dressed as jockeys. The undisputed doyen of this last group was Ras Prince Monolulu (right), a giant of a man who had been a decade or more in the business before his tip of 100–6 outsider *Spion Kop* (which won the 1920 Derby in a record time that held for sixteen years) made him famous. His shout of 'I gotta horse' and his towering feathered head-dress ensured that no one missed him! I once saw him about to board the Epsom train at Victoria, and have wondered ever since how he coped with those feathers in the railway carriage. He remained a feature of many race meetings after the Second World War and died in February 1965, aged about eighty.

Postwar racing. The end of the Second World War found the course in a sorry state, with bomb craters, blast damage and chunks of concrete debris littering the terraces of the grandstand. Thanks to a great job of patching, make-do and mend with the materials available, it made ready to receive visitors, hungry for another sign of a return to normal after the vicissitudes of wartime. With the traditional royal drive down the course amid roars of loyal welcome for King George VI and Queen Elizabeth, the Derby was staged again at Epsom in 1946. It was won by *Airborne* at 50–1 by one length, a close finish by a long shot, adding drama to the high excitement of the day. 1954 saw the first Derby win by Lester Piggott, then eighteen years old, on 33–1 *Never Say Die*. In the 1962 race, a fallen horse brought down six others; extricated from the heaving mass, 22–1 *Larkspur* (sired by *Never Say Die*) went on to win the race.

Jockey Charles Smirke. Charlie was apprenticed to Epsom trainer Stanley Wootton and by the age of twenty was already engaged to ride for some prestigious owners. In 1934 he won the Derby by a length on *Windsor Lad*, equalling the course record of 2 minutes 34 seconds. Two years later he rode *Mahmoud* to victory for the Aga Khan at 100–8, knocking 0.5 seconds off that record. 'What did I *Tulyar*?' Charlie announced on the eve of the 1952 Derby – and won again for the Aga Khan on the 11–2 favourite of that name. Six years later, at the age of fifty-one, he won by five lengths on *Hard Ridden* for Sir Victor Sassoon. In the original of this cigarette card portrait, he is wearing the Aga Khan's colours of green and chocolate brown.

Special raceday buses. After the Second World War and the return of the Derby to Epsom (it was run at Newmarket from 1940 to 1945) huge crowds supported the race meetings. Shortages meant there were not yet many private motor cars, but the London Underground system could bring racegoers from anywhere in the metropolis to the terminus at Morden, where double-decker buses waited to convey them direct to the course. Other 'specials' met rail travellers at Epsom station, while those arriving at Epsom Downs or Tattenham Corner stations found themselves on the spot.

Epsom Racing Lads' Club. In April 1949, after conversion from a private house, The Uplands, 19 Downs Road, was opened as a club for all local stable lads under twenty-three. It was the brainchild of trainer Stanley Wootton's secretary, Mr E.H. Groves, supported by Epsom trainers and other interested

parties. They realised that the youngsters, living in hostels or lodgings and involved with their horses in the early mornings and late afternoons, had time on their hands and nowhere to spend it. Democratically run by its 130 members, the club had facilities for boxing and gymnastics (with changing rooms and showers), snooker, darts and table tennis, and fielded three football teams. Refreshments were available whenever the club was open. The gym (above †) had been created from a row of six loose-boxes in the grounds, and it was here (in the boxing ring!) in 1953 that I helped start the judo section of the club (see p. 99). A bi-monthly magazine the *Uplands Review* was edited by John Sheear, pictured here on the right, with fellow-lad Ron Stewart in Peter Thrale's yard.

Plain Jane. In the yard of Peter Thrale's Beaconsfield Road training establishment, stable lad Ron Stewart rides his favourite charge, *Plain Jane*. Other Epsom trainers were Vic Smythe, Walter Nightingall (in Burgh Heath Road) who trained the 1943 Newmarket Derby winner *Straight Deal* for Mrs Dorothy Paget, Stanley Wootton, Tommy Gosling and Staff Ingham.

Golden Sally, 1951. In the 1950 season *Golden Sally*, trained at Epsom by Stanley Wootton (here with D.J. Savage), finished in the first four in nine races, including Newmarket and the Stud Produce Stakes at Sandown Park. †

The Drift Bridge Hotel. Occasionally this hotel was the venue for fund-raising dances and other events for the Racing Lads' Club. On 6 November 1951 a different kind of celebration took place there, when Peter Thrale's stable saluted the triumph of their *Three Cheers* in winning the Cesarewich. Mr Thrale himself, the owner Mr C. Payne Crofts and jockeys Ken Gethin, Manny Mercer and Charlie Smirke were among the celebrities who signed the souvenir menu (below) which, not surprisingly, was set out in the style of a race card.

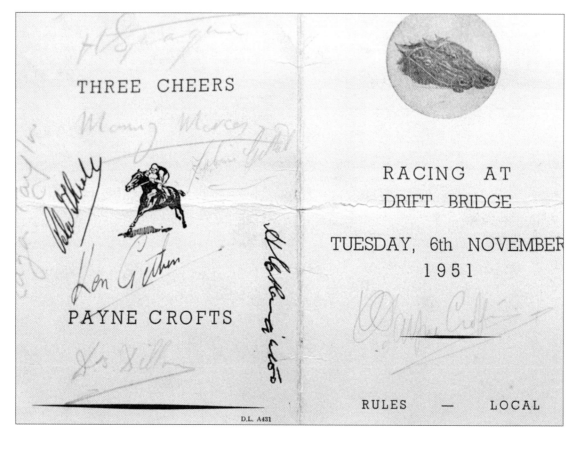

Show-Out Sunday, 1956. For generations the Sunday before Derby week has traditionally seen thousands of people converging on the racecourse to sample the delights of sideshows and entertainers, fortune-tellers and fairground rides. Calm and respectful in the midst of all the revelry, some would attend a religious service, complete with sermon by a bishop or other worthy. In 1956 a local newspaper reported that 'hot dogs with onions were very popular' with the crowd, and the weather was kind (though few shirtsleeves or cotton dresses can be seen here). An augmented bus service from Epsom railway station ran to capacity from early in the day. Though private cars were not as plentiful as in later years, those that did attend added to a grand evening snarl-up at the Spread Eagle crossroads. Together with buses and motor coaches, they streamed down from the racecourse, meeting an equal volume of traffic returning from a day at the coast. *

The Rubbing House (formerly Downs House). Little changed architecturally, the public house once run by Mr Edward Clark (see p. 56) has now reverted to its original name and vividly evokes the early days of horse-racing on the Downs, when contests were run in heats over a four-mile course. Setting off from a point near Banstead village, a horse might be required to run the distance as many as four times in one day (not counting the slower return journeys to the start). A break at the end of each heat allowed thirty minutes to give the horses a breather while being rubbed down. An eighteenth-century wooden building for this purpose, which inspired the original name, burned down in 1857. Its replacement survives to this day.

The Queen's stand. This 'glass palace' of a stand opened in 1992, with the very latest in hospitality suites and other accommodation. Prompted by such innovations, the racecourse management added some evening meetings to their summer schedule.

Visitors, November 1996. Hands are raised in amazement and delight as visitors to the Derby Experience guided tour get their first view of the course from the Queen's stand. Other features of the visit included time in the weighing room, where one could be photographed seated on the scales (with weight prominently displayed!).

4

West Side

Dorking Road, 1929. This postcard view of the road across the common between Epsom and Ashtead was published by Wells & Son of High Street, Epsom. Their premises, near Waterloo House (Assembly Rooms, p. 29) seem to have been one of the early eighteenth-century shops built of wood with only the façade of brick. This was the latest fashion, which was elsewhere satisfied by the use of mathematical tiles, as seen on houses in Ewell village. In Victorian times an iron sunblind-style canopy supported on openwork twisted posts was added. This was also the location of the Rosary Tea Gardens. A scheme to build a road to by-pass Ashtead village to the east of the Dorking Road near Ashtead Park was first put forward not long after the end of the Second World War. It came up for discussion periodically over the next thirty years before final rejection. The M25 motorway, passing quite close to the south of the village, was opened in 1985.

Baron's Pond, 1900. The pond, on the common to the west of Wilmerhatch Lane, was named after the eighteenth Baron de Tessier of Woodcote Park. In the 1970s the combined efforts of the Parks Department of the local authority and concerned volunteers cleared and revitalised the neglected pond.

Horton Lane, 1903. Grazing cattle, milk pails on the dairyman's yoke – a scene little changed from the days two hundred years earlier when Samuel Pepys wrote in his diary about Mr Minnes who owned Horton and Woodcote Park (see p. 73). Mr Minnes' daughter Elizabeth was married to Richard, brother of diarist John Evelyn.

Woodcote Pond, *c.* 1911. The trees are a reminder that woodland once covered this part of Epsom; it is easy to see why a separate settlement grew up here in medieval times, and why a pond was created for its use. The fortunes of the pond have waxed and waned, but care and appreciation of it have increased in recent years. This view, looking north-east along Woodcote Green Road, was published by A. Jones of Ivey's Retreat in South Street.

Corner of Stamford Pond, looking east, 1911. Here is the first of the ponds on the common as one leaves the town, in the area where legend has it that Mr Wicker's cow in 1618 stumbled upon a puddle of purgative water that turned Epsom into the country's earliest spa. The central building (behind the trees), Kingswood House School, stands on the site of the home of 'Colonel' Kelly, owner of wonder horse *Eclipse*. Past the house and on to the crest of West Hill, a magnificent view across the town and beyond is afforded with, on the left, a public house named after that great horse, whose offspring won the second-ever Derby in 1781 (*Young Eclipse*), the 1783 race (*Saltram*) and the 1784 (*Sergeant*). His line can be traced in many other Derby winners.

Dorking Road, 1915. The road from the town centre to the original wells was planted with elms and lime trees in about 1700, creating an attractive route for the fashionable visitors making their way to take the waters. Later, many of the trees were cut down, but one or two survived into the twentieth century. When Mr James Gubbins lived at Hylands (opposite White Horse Drive) he was several times (between 1805 and 1811) visited by his nephew by marriage, artist John Constable, whose oil painting of Epsom Common is in the National Gallery. In 1825, at nearby Woodmansterne, the artist was a guest of the Lambert family, who had commissioned a portrait. Later artists associated with Epsom included Augustus John and Aubrey Beardsley.

The Stew Pond, *c.* 1925. When, in medieval times, the common land was under the jurisdiction of the Abbot of Chertsey, this artificially created fish pond was of great benefit to the monks. Stocked with carp and other fish, it yielded fresh food in winter, and year-round meals for their meatless Fridays. Reminiscers recall the days when the one-acre pond, lined with clay and fed by local streams, froze over and skaters arrived, plus an enterprising trader who cut and stored blocks of ice for later use. At other times the pond could deteriorate into a marshy hollow, but later historians and conservationists came to appreciate its importance and that of its neighbour, the six-acre Great Pond. A major project of repairs and restoration took place, largely the work of volunteers under the aegis of the Epsom Common Association, formed in 1974. Winner of a commendation from the Civic Trust in 1980, this lovely area continues to attract wildlife and human visitors.

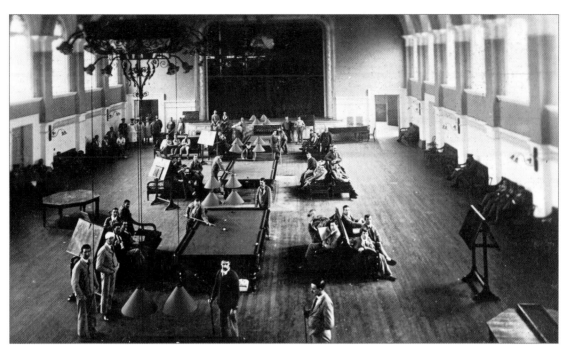

County of London War Hospitals. Horton Hospital (above), built to house London County Council mental patients, was used during the First World War as a convalescent hospital for the Blue Boys, so-called from the shapeless bright-blue suits they dressed in (sometimes with regimental headgear). Featured here is the soldier's recreation room with billiard tables and other available facilities, including a stage. At that time, the Manor Hospital (below), a postcard view published by L.W. Andrews & Son (see p. 14), was similarly used.

In the Second World War, Horton once again received wounded troops, though some civilian surgical patients were accommodated. While my grandfather was thus cared for, a number of soldiers were brought in, one of whom I was sent across to talk to whenever too many family came to see Gramp. The lad's condition deteriorated rapidly until the day came when he lapsed into a coma and all I could do for him was sit at his bedside. A nurse gently led me away: he had died as I held his hand. I was fourteen.

The Farm Camp, Woodcote, 1919. This separate area began service in the First World War as a camp for reserve troops, but later became part of the Canadian Army convalescent camp. At the date of this photograph the war was over but many frustrated colonial troops waited for ships to take them home. Late on the night of 17 June 1919 a group of Canadians laid siege to the Ashley Road police station (p. 30), where two comrades were detained after trouble in the town. Thirteen of the twenty-four police defenders were hurt in the attack that followed, and station sergeant Thomas Green died.

Rosebery Park, 1930s. Lord Rosebery gave the eleven-acre site to the town in 1913. Young trees were planted, paths laid and benches set out, in time for this green spot to serve as a quiet meeting-place for the hundreds of First World War convalescent soldiers encamped nearby (see p. 105). Not long after this view was included in a lettercard, the park featured in the 1937 Charter celebrations (see pp. 107–8). Public dancing to the Dix Dance Band (under the direction of Mr R. Harvey) took place from 7.30 to 10 p.m. on Saturday 2 October – 'all welcome'. Open air dances were popular in the 1930s and '40s, but normally in the summer months!

Rosebery Park. A few new seats, taller trees and a more relaxed feel to the dress and attitudes of the folk frequenting the park – these are the only noticeable changes in the tranquil scene over a forty-year period. Compare child-minding techniques with page 77, however! In the '50s, movie cameras came to the park to film for *Sailor Beware!* which starred the late Peggy Mount (who did not, however, appear in the scene of a courting couple on a bench by the pond). Drama of another sort occurred when all the ornamental fish disappeared from that pond; an angler was engaged, and he eventually landed a rogue pike that had been living very well indeed.

West Park Hospital. The hospital's 1956 sports day and prize-giving took place in June. Eight trainee nurses, including three male students, received awards, watched by their colleagues and distinguished guests, the Mayor and Mayoress of Epsom, Councillor and Mrs W.J. Clark, the Mayor and Mayoress of Mitchem, Councillor and Mrs H.T. Longshaw, and Dr P.J. Watkins and Mrs S.B. Samuels, respectively chairman and vice chairman of the hospital management committee. *

Rosebery Park, 1997. Mercifully the park itself remains much as it was fifty years ago, when I first enjoyed its quiet walks and noble trees. Mothers still take their toddlers to watch the wildfowl on the pond; workers still sprawl on the grass in their lunch-hour; youngsters still hurtle along the paths, but today with their roller-blades and skateboards rather than the dollies' prams and soapbox go-karts of yesteryear.

The old well on the common, 1980s. Landscaped and crowned with a wrought-iron frame and lamp, the site of the well was blessed by the Vicar of Christ Church, the Revd Mark Wilson, in a ceremony on 25 June 1989. A plaque records how the medicinal waters found there in the seventeenth century made Epsom the country's first spa town.

5

Schools & Colleges

Epsom College athletes. Established at the south-east end of Alexandra Road in 1851 by 'poor Welsh apothecary' John Lumsden Probert, the college placed much importance on sport. Surrounding head prefect F. McNield and photographed by Mr C.H. Hopkins (see p. 104), students represent hockey, fives, athletics, cricket, gymnastics and football.

Epsom College. John Probert started his Royal Medical Benevolent College with one hundred pupils and twenty-four pensioners and dependants (including children, for whom he provided a playground). These two views were sent in 1902 to one young postcard enthusiast by another who recorded that she then held in her collection '977 not counting swaps, 1,004 counting them'.

The Chapel, Epsom College. The chapel was among the first buildings erected on land given by Dr Graham of Epsom. Albert, the Prince Consort, had performed the opening ceremony accompanied by his son Prince Edward who, forty years later, attended the foundation of the Lower School.

The Chemistry Laboratory, Epsom College, 1924. Originally a medical foundation, the College expected many of its pupils to go on to train as doctors: laboratories were therefore essential. Founder John Probert had trained at St Bartholomew's and went into practice in 1814. Born in Cardiganshire, at the age of fifteen he took part in the Napoleonic wars.

Actor Stewart Granger (1913–93). Following preparatory school, where he was champion boxer at the age of ten, James Lablanche Stewart (Granger's real name) attended Epsom College. He left at sixteen-and-a-half, having won colours for swimming and rugby football. Work as a film extra led to two years' study at the Webber Douglas Academy of Dramatic Art, followed by repertory at Hull and Birmingham, a Malvern Festival, an Old Vic tour, and several feature film rôles. After war service in the Black Watch and ENSA, a leading part in *The Man in Grey* (1943) assured his success with home audiences. He starred in some forty movies in the UK and in the United States, and towards the end of his life made a welcome return to the London stage. Other celebrities educated at the College were novelist Francis Brett Young (winner of the first Rosebery Prize for English Literature in 1895), and artists Graham Sutherland and John Piper (see p. 102).

From the air, 1924. 'K', a college pupil, sent this aerial view 'taken last term' to his mother in December 1924. There is little news about school work, but he expands on plans for a school excursion to Richard III at the Old Vic in the Christmas holidays.

Rosebery School for Girls, 1939. High jinks at the school's sports day – enough to distract one spectator from the race in progress. The school badge incorporates a primrose, recalling Lord Rosebery's family name.

Epsom College, 1955. As part of the College's centenary celebrations Her Majesty the Queen, accompanied by the Duke of Edinburgh, maintained the College's royal connections with a visit. In chairs on the pavement opposite the College gates, warmly clad and blanketed, residents of The Firs old people's home waved small Union flags at Her Majesty (and each other) as the royal procession drove in. By 1962 there were some five hundred boys aged between twelve and nineteen on the College roll. *

Ruxley Lane School. Above is the junior football team that represented the school in 1955. Seated right is Mr Victor Blore, who in his playing days before joining the school staff kept goal for West Ham and Crystal Palace. In the 1950s a large contingent of pupils (below) embarked on a group holiday. Since 1978 the school has been known as Epsom and Ewell High School.

Rosebery School, 1950s. The girls' school in White Horse Drive was officially opened on 24 November 1921, with Mrs Skeats JP performing the ceremony. In the next thirty years the number of pupils increased to such an extent that the assembly hall was not large enough to accommodate students, parents and guests, for prize-givings. In the early '50s, the event took place at the Baths Hall, East Street, Epsom.

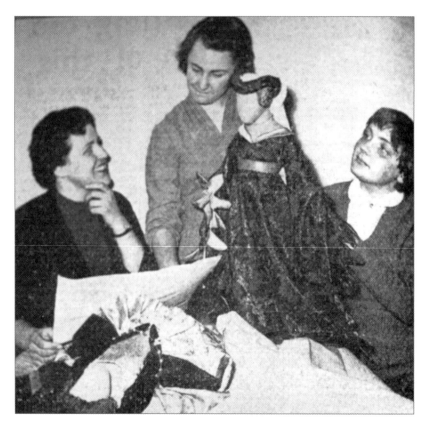

Epsom School of Art, April 1956. The department of dress design included in its syllabus a study of historic costume. Left to right: Myril Smith, Christine Taylor and Jean Morgan are comparing an original design with a small-scale copy. *

Ewell Technical College, 1956. At the College's Building Department prize-giving (above), Sir Graham Savage (right) spoke of the need to upgrade the industry from a trade to a profession. Mr F.W. Horrobin, head of the department, reported one hundred per cent success in the City and Guilds final examination and ninety-eight per cent in the intermediate. Below, Rodney Jones (left) and Roger Burton put into practice some of the brickwork course skills they had acquired. *

Nonsuch County School for Girls. Miss Marion M. Dickie, MA, was the first headmistress of the school, which opened in 1938. The full complement of pupils had not been reached at the outbreak of the Second World War (the most senior being the Fourth Form), when large numbers of children were evacuated to safer areas of the country and to far-flung parts of the Empire. Many lessons were held in air raid shelters built in the grounds. Miss Dickie retired in 1964. She was succeeded by Miss J.W. Matthews, MA (left). *

In 1981 Miss Dickie returned to Nonsuch to meet more than three hundred former pupils, celebrating her eightieth birthday. About to cut her cake (right), she paused to deliver a few pithy responses to the greetings of her girls (the oldest at that time aged about fifty-seven). She died four years later, and many of us reconvened at a service of thanksgiving at St Andrew's United Reformed Church, Northey Avenue. Our first head girl, Myfanwy Rowlands (Mrs M. Piggott, MA), spoke for us all in her tribute to Nonsuch's first headmistress.

6
Sport & Leisure

Bicycling. When the twentieth century dawned, bicycles were the sport and the transport of the masses. Clubs were formed and excursions arranged from city centres into the countryside on Sundays (most people worked a five-and-a-half or six-day week). Epsom Downs and Ashtead Woods (see p. 116) were popular destinations for Londoners (a thirty-mile round trip). Shops and repair depots sprang up along all routes, and in Epsom, Mr Page (Waterloo Road), Mr Hersey (South Street) and Mr Absalom did a brisk trade. Many an inn and tearoom advertised its willingness to cater for tired and famished riders.

The Golf House, Epsom Downs, 1910. Epsom Golf Club was formed in May 1889, although it is believed that some form of the game was being played on the Downs nearly a century earlier. The clubhouse, opened in 1892, was designed by local man J. Hatchard Smith, whose other work included Epsom Public Hall (see p. 93) and the Trocadero Hotel in London's West End. Although ladies were admitted as associate members as early as 1909, they were not allowed to use the clubhouse until fifty-one years later, having had their own small premises nearby in the interim.

The Cedars, Church Street. The 1st Epsom (St Martin's) Girl Guide company first met in 1919 in the grounds of this house, once the home of Mary Moffat, wife of Dr David Livingstone, Victorian explorer and missionary. The house became a school, where their children were educated. The hurricane of 1987 destroyed the magnificent trees from which the house took its name.

The Capitol Cinema, Church Road, 1930s. One of the first in a chain of cinemas established by the Wainwright family, the Capitol, seating over 1,500, was opened on Monday, 30 December 1929, by Lord Ebbisham, Member of Parliament for Epsom from 1918 to 1924 and Lord Mayor of London, 1926 to 1927. Among the distinguished guests was Commander A.R.J. Southey, who had become Epsom's MP in 1928. The house beyond the cinema, 6 Church Road, was occupied by Mr R.B. Wainwright and his family. Though in the next decade movie audiences came to expect glamorous and colourful surroundings in their cinemas, in 1929 the Capitol must have seemed a veritable dream. The walls, pillars, ceiling and proscenium arch were in delicate pastel colours, highlighted with silver; the highly successful café was also used for *thé dansants*, receptions and other functions. The Public Hall (far left) built in 1883, after thirty-three years as a men's social club (ground floor) and auditorium (upstairs) for all manner of entertainments and meetings, came to house the Picture Palladium, whose first shows included footage of the war in France. Its demise coincided with the success of the Capitol.

EPSOM, COURT RECREATION GROUND.   74096

Court Recreation Ground, Pound Lane. This twenty-one-acre site was acquired for public use by purchase (1924 and 1928) of parts of the Court Farm estate and the grounds of seventeenth-century West Hill House. It comprised tennis courts, bowling and putting greens as well as open playing-fields with pavilions, flower-beds and children's corner. The postcard from which the above view is taken was posted in Epsom in July 1943 and includes the comment 'The scenery round here is lovely, what a treat not to see any damage. Have forgotten all about the war'.

In the early 1950s, a new sport was introduced at the recreation ground when Epsom Lions baseball team set out their diamond. Founded by Canadians and Americans living locally, the vociferous game soon attracted spectators (left), some of them keen to understand the rules, others who went on to become players. Visiting teams included Kodak, United States Air Force (Bushey Park) and United States Navy (London). Lions team members and their supporters travelled to away games in Richmond's coaches.

Epsom Girl Guides, 1950s. A grand parade of the town's Guides was lined up on the forecourt of St Martin's Parish Church. Although the apparently inclement weather resulted in a variety of outer clothing, one cannot fail to be impressed by the uniform display of white ankle socks. All North Surrey Guides assembled at the racecourse for a rally in 1957, attended by the Chief Guide, Lady Baden-Powell, widow of the founder of the Boy Scout movement. Below: Lady Baden-Powell sends some words of encouragement to the Guides.

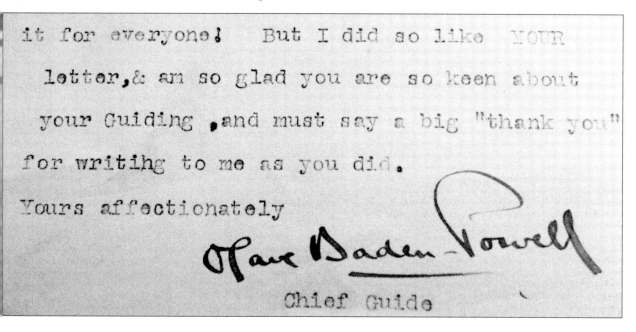

Song of Norway. Epsom Operatic and Dramatic Society presented this musical play at the Ebbisham Hall, Ashley Road, in February 1954. The main parts were played by Rex Baines, Susan Gray, Bryn Jones, Hilda Lambolle and John Furniss, who also devised the ballet sequences. Other 1950s productions included *Rose Marie, Balalaika, Perchance to Dream* and *Show Boat.* The Operatic Society's first production in March 1911 was *The Mountaineers,* followed in 1912 by Gilbert and Sullivan's *The Mikado* (in aid of Dr Barnardo's Home in East Street) and in 1913 *The Gondoliers* (proceeds to local charities) – all at the Public Hall.

Those were the days, 1950. Perhaps as a reaction to the casual style of wartime dancing – jitterbug, jive and so on – the late 1940s saw the rise of old-time dancing, with its formal dress and courtesies. All ages took to the floor for the Valeta, Empress Tango, Moonlight Saunter and Military Two-Step, while groups of friends regularly joined together in set dances like the Lancers. Dancers from the youth clubs of which I was a member in those days travelled all over Surrey to support these events, where Sydney Thompson and his orchestra often played. They broadcast each Saturday evening from the BBC studio in London's Regent Street, and we went there too.

Football: Epsom versus Tooting and Mitcham. On a misty Saturday in January 1956, Epsom players were away to Tooting and Mitcham for a Surrey Senior Cup quarter-final. The visitors were plagued by injuries, and the home team was expected to win by five goals. Good defensive work by Epsom goalkeeper Butler (described by a reporter as 'confidence itself'), Nuth and Reynolds kept down Tooting's score, but Epsom's Wales ('an artistic player'), Purkiss, Murphy ('his ultra-short shorts would have made a continental blush') and the rest could do no more and they lost the match 2–0. Epsom men (in quartered shirts) pictured above, left to right: Bill Nuth, Bill Purkiss and Bernard Wales with Don Butler (goalkeeper). *

Netball. In the 1956 District Youth League championship, the girls of Epsom Methodist Youth Club emerged winners for the second year. In all games played, they scored a total of over two hundred goals, while conceding ninety. Left to right, front row: L. Bray, team captain B. Bourne, J. Bourne; back row: F. Uren, P. Timson, A. Fowler, S. Ford. *

Pantomimes, January 1956. As well as professional shows staged at local theatres and cinemas, amateur groups put on seasonal entertainments. *Sutton & Cheam Advertiser's* edition of Thursday, 12 January contained the above picture of members of the Club Players from Stoneleigh Residents' Tennis and Social Club who appeared in *Mother Goose*. At Epsom's Horton Hospital, the drama section of the Sports Club gave three performances of *Humpty Dumpty*. Directed by Peter Bazeley, the cast included (below) Mr J. Fuscoe as the wizard, with Vera Harris (who also arranged the dances) and Pat L'Aquilar. *

Opposite: Granada cinema, Church Street, 1956. In 1947 the Capitol cinema (see p. 93) was acquired by Granada Theatres Limited, and changed its name. In spite of a promotional jingle something like 'It isn't any harder to say Granada', for a long time devoted supporters continued to use the old, more exclusive, title. (Children attending Saturday morning shows at a neighbouring cinema built in earlier days by the same group had no such difficulty: their anthem – to the tune of 'Funiculi, Funicula' – was 'Granada! Granada! London Road, North Cheam!'). All manner of show business folk made 'personal appearances' to boost their forthcoming movies, and many publicity stunts were staged (see pp. 102 and 111). It is interesting to note the relative 'draw' attached at the time to the films showing in the week of 11 June: Marilyn Monroe's name is in the smaller print. *

In aid of the stable lads. A fund-raising day for Epsom Racing Lads' Club (see p. 66) was held at the football ground, West Street, Ewell, in May 1955. It included a display of unarmed combat (self-defence) devised by the colleague with whom I helped organise the judo section of the club. Here I am (in tartan trews) preparing the arena surrounded by mystified but friendly onlookers. I was no judo expert, but my Black Belt 'attacker' made me look good as I repeatedly threw him to the ground, with his show of agonised screams and pleas for mercy.

Sporting activities, summer 1956. The Surrey County trials for women bowlers were held on the fine Cumberland turf greens of Epsom Bowling Club in Worple Road (above). Over at the county track in Motspur Park, an Epsom College athlete, M. Prior, took part in the junior javelin event during the Surrey Athletic Championship (left). *

Mr John Clifford Gale, principal conductor of the Epsom Symphony Orchestra. The orchestra evolved in 1947 from a small group of chamber musicians. Four years later the number had grown sufficiently to form the Epsom Concert Orchestra which, in coronation year 1953, became the Epsom Symphony Orchestra Society. By 1959 Gale was principal conductor and also chairman of the society. Concerts were given at the Baths Hall and the Ebbisham Hall in Epsom, and at other venues including the Baths Hall, Malden Road, North Cheam. Soloists of the calibre of pianist Peter Katin were engaged to perform with the orchestra; local girl Kathleen Riddick also conducted. In November 1963, under Mr Gale's baton, local singers and musicians gave one performance of Mozart's *The Magic Flute*.

RAC Country Club. Standing in its 300-acre grounds used for the previous twenty years by the Royal Automobile Club as its country club, on 1 August 1934 this mid-eighteenth-century mansion at Woodcote Park was destroyed by fire. Within two years a new house stood on the site. With panoramic views of the surrounding countryside, the celebrated golf course attracts top players and competitors: the first UK Bob Hope Classic was held there. This view is from a publicity postcard which proclaims that the house was 'painted with Berger Paints'.

Richard Attenborough, 1960. *The Angry Silence* was a serious film treatment of workers' strikes and lock-outs; while it was showing at Epsom's Granada its star, Richard Attenborough, made a personal appearance (he and co-producer Bryan Forbes later received an Oscar nomination). After a decade of youthful rôles this was a turning-point in Attenborough's career. His later mature portrayals in *The League of Gentlemen*, *The Great Escape* and *10 Rillington Place* among others led him to the heights in movie production and eventual worldwide acclaim (*Oh! What a Lovely War!*, *Gandhi*, etc.). Few who heard him that day at the Granada could have foreseen his knighthood and other honours.

Odeon cinema, Upper High Street, 2001. Epsom was without an Odeon for nigh on thirty years, after its first (in the High Street) closed in June 1971 (see p. 29). Today's building stands close to the site of the Lecture Hall, erected in 1883 for the Sunday School department of the Congregational church, which survived, though derelict, into the 1990s. I remember the 'concertina' iron lattice gates closed across a shabby entrance, depository for all manner of rubbish, a sad end to a hall that had been the setting for a wide variety of amateur shows. As a young man, artist and stage designer John Piper, living in Ashley Road and once a day-boy at Epsom College (see pp. 81–6), painted back-cloths for Lecture Hall shows, and was also pianist with a small group that played for dances and entertainments. His *Ruins of St Mary le Port* was chosen for the 1s 6d postage stamp in a British Paintings series in 1968, alongside works by John Constable (see p. 74) and Sir Thomas Lawrence.

7
Residents & Visitors

Mr Robert Dearle, c. 1904. Mr Dearle is standing outside the shop at 100 High Street, established by his father at the end of the eighteenth century. A chandler and oilman, Mr Dearle manufactured candles and soap from tallow in the workshop at the rear. By the time he died in 1906, it was his proud boast that he had attended eighty successive runnings of the Derby, without ever placing a bet on the race.

Sir Ernest H. Shackleton, CVO. Hero of polar explorations, Sir Ernest came to Epsom to present his lecture *Nearest the South Pole* (with Kinematograph pictures) at the Public Hall on 15 March 1910, at the invitation of the Epsom and District Literary Society. Tickets were priced at *7s 6d* and *5s 0d* for reserved seats and *2s 6d* for unreserved (a limited number); they could be purchased from Andrews' Library (see p. 14). This doughty Irishman had reached within one hundred miles of the Pole on his 1907–9 expedition, returning in 1914. He died in the Antarctic in 1922, while undertaking scientific work there.

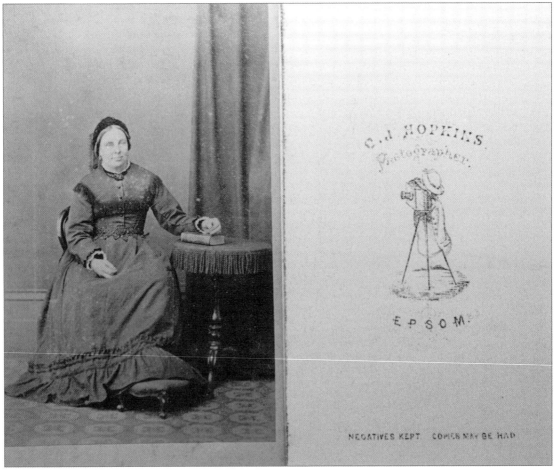

Carte de visite. The two sides of this card publicise the work of Mr C.J. Hopkins of Hampden House, Epsom, who also photographed the College group on p. 81. Other early local practitioners of the new form of portraiture were Mr J.G. Tillett of The Studio, Church Street, Mr Mills (High Street) and Mr A.E. Long.

Convalescent Canadian soldiers, 1916. 'The King and Queen came here today' is part of the message dated 18 July 1916 written on the back of the postcard view of part of the three-quarters of a mile main avenue through Woodcote Park camp (above), in use by February 1915 for training grounds. Within a few months the site had become a convalescent camp for Empire troops (as many as four thousand at times) returning wounded from the battlefronts of the First World War. The royal visit was the official opening of the camp's recreation hall (below). Both viewcards are from the series sold in Canadian YMCA canteens.

Councillor the Revd Edward Earle Dorling, MA, FSA. At the time of Epsom's charter celebrations in 1937, Mr Dorling lived in Alexandra Road. He was elected Third Substitute Mayor and, jointly with First Substitute Mayor, Councillor John Samuel Underhill (Chairman of the Urban District Council), donated the Common Seal of the corporation to commemorate the event.

He also designed the new arms of the borough (right), which are used to this day. His aim was to celebrate 'the leading industry of the neighbourhood', hence the golden equine heads on a green field (for horse-racing and training), with the blue waves of water for Ewell's sparkling streams – or perhaps as a reminder of Epsom's former greatness through its wells – and white for the chalk of the Downs. King Henry VIII's long-vanished palace at the eastern extreme of the borough is remembered in the motto.

James Chuter Ede (1882–1965), Epsom's Charter Mayor, 1937. Each time I saw him in the town, though honours came his way for his lifelong public service – Privy Councillor, Companion of Honour, a Baronetcy – this true son of Epsom seemed to retain the common touch with his fellow citizens. From elementary education at the local national school, by way of the high school in Dorking and teaching college, he came home from Christ's College, Cambridge, to teach in Ewell. After service with the East Surreys in the First World War, he stood unsuccessfully as Labour candidate for Epsom in the 1918 election. At his next attempt in 1923 he was elected to represent Mitcham, and thus began an illustrious political career. He was deeply involved in the preparation of the Education Act of 1944, served as Home Secretary under Attlee from 1945 to 1951, and was for a time Leader of the House. He was among the guests of honour at the official opening of Nonsuch County School for Girls on 20 June 1938; when the following summer I won a scholarship to the school, my father needed a reference from a person of standing to back his claim for exemption from some of the fees. Mr (as he was then) Chuter Ede obliged, and I have always felt my fine education owed something to that kind gentleman. His home was at Tayles Hill, Ewell.

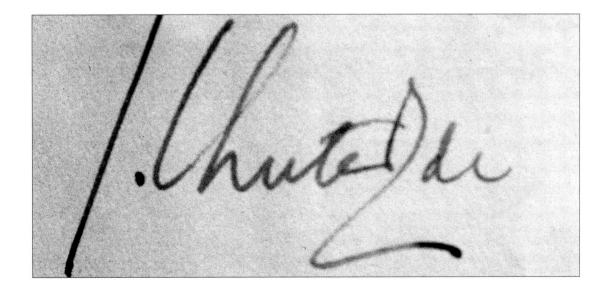

The Charter Mayoress. Mrs J. Chuter Ede began her official duties on 29 September 1937 at 8.15 a.m. by laying wreaths at the Garden of Remembrance, Ewell churchyard, and the War Memorial, Ashley Road, Epsom. Her last engagement that day, at her husband's side, was to accompany the Lord Lieutenant, High Sheriff and other distinguished guests from the Mansion House, Nonsuch Park (where proceedings to celebrate the official opening of the park ended at 5.50 p.m.) to the Dorking Road boundary of the new borough. The Mayoress's new chain and badge were commemorative gifts from the Surrey Trainers' Association.

The Charter Town Clerk. 'Philip Edward Whiteoak-Cooper, a solicitor of the Supreme Court and Commissioner for Oaths, Clerk of the Urban District Council of Epsom and Ewell' (according to the Charter of Incorporation of the Borough of Epsom and Ewell, 29 September 1937) was the first appointed Town Clerk of the new borough. He and Mrs Whiteoak-Cooper travelled in the third carriage in the procession leaving the Town Hall at 8.50 a.m. on the morning of the great day. They toured the district as far as the Mansion House, Nonsuch Park, and were back at Epsom Clock Tower in time for the presentation of the charter at twelve noon.

Two stars. Local residents and star entertainers Ralph Lynn (1882–1962, left) and Tom Walls (1883–1949) first appeared together in the farce *Tons of Money* (737 performances) in 1923 and continued the partnership of 'thirteen successes in thirteen years' (Tom's lucky number) with the so-called Aldwych farces. These included Ben Travers' plays *A Cuckoo in the Nest*, *Rookery Nook*, *Plunder* and others. For the former railway worker and Metropolitan policeman, Tom Walls, the lure of the turf eventually outdid that of the footlights: he turned away from the movies in the 1930s. From his stables at North Looe, Reigate Road, he produced the 1932 Derby winner *April the Fifth*, one of the very few owner-trained horses to win the modern event. At about this time, my grandfather received a half-crown (2s 6d) gratuity from Mr Walls, for stopping another of his horses bolting along the road. Ralph Lynn, who lived in Wilmerhatch Lane and later moved to Tadworth, had played in musical comedies opposite such stars as Evelyn Laye and Binnie Hale before joining Tom, Yvonne Arnaud and Robertson Hare in the 1923 farce. After some years in movies he returned to the West End stage in 1944, keeping audiences happy in hazardous wartime London with *Is your honeymoon really necessary?* In April 1937, Epsom's latest thing in cinemas, the Odeon (see p. 29), was officially opened by these two popular actors, before more than one thousand admirers.

Derek McCulloch of the BBC (1897–1967). From the 1930s he lived in Nork, and it was close to his home in April 1938 that he was involved in a traffic accident which led to the amputation of his left leg, with much subsequent pain and difficulty with an artificial limb. Having been wounded in the First World War (he joined the Public Schools Battalion at the age of seventeen and transferred to the Royal Flying Corps in 1917), he endured many operations. He was with the BBC from 1926 and became a member of the popular *Children's Hour* team seven years later, in which he was 'Uncle Mac', beloved of thousands of young listeners. One Oaks Day (when I should have been in college) I came face to face with him on the racecourse: emboldened by my win of ten shillings on the big race, I asked for his autograph. Though ill-at-ease and walking on the rough grass with difficulty, the kind man obliged. A decade later he unwittingly helped me again: I was married in the same church and on the same day as his daughter, and had the benefit of her floral decorations.
(The portrait (left) comes from a Wills cigarette card.)

Jimmy Edwards. This popular comedian, probably best remembered for his radio and television work in *Take it from here*, *Whacko!*, other comedies and panel games, made a personal appearance at the Granada (p. 99) in July 1952. He was promoting his movie *Treasure Hunt* in which he starred with two grande-dames of stage and screen, Martita Hunt and Athene Seyler.

Below: Off-duty stable lads. Out of work-clothes and in their Sunday best, here are pals Ron Stewart and Kevin Spence (known as Spike) snapped on the Downs near Mr Thrale's Beaconsfield Road premises. As ever, the grandstand's prominent siting stands as a constant reminder of what Epsom is all about.

Councillor H.W. Cushine JP (1899–1963). Mr Bill Cushine was a founder-pupil of Pound Lane School, which opened in 1907. He was Chairman of the old Epsom Urban District Council from 1934 to 1935, and Mayor from 1938 to 1939, when one of his engagements was the official opening of the Baths Hall in East Street. Among his other important contributions to the life of the community was negotiating the acquisition of twenty-one acres of the former Epsom Court estate and their transformation into the Court Recreation Ground (see p. 94). He was a familiar figure in the town in the early 1950s, a highly respected 'local boy who made good'.

WI fashion show, 1956. At the May meeting of Langley Vale Women's Institute there was a display of fashions and millinery created and modelled by the members themselves. They included Mrs Lunn, Mrs Mallinson and Mrs Meadows. *

Off to Canada. Mrs Isobel Evans, well-known for her work for the British Legion in Epsom, left her home town in May 1956 to live in Canada. Accompanied by her son-in-law, daughter and granddaughter, Mr and Mrs Maurice Burford and Valerie, she would be reunited with another daughter, Phyllis, who went to Canada in 1946. *

PETULA CLARK

Exclusive **Pye-Nixa** Recording Artist

Singer/actress Petula Clark. Child star Petula, born in Salmons Road, Chessington, in 1932, caught the nation's attention when she was heard on the wireless, sending a message in song to a serving soldier during the Second World War. She was already well known locally for her performances with the restaurant orchestra at Bentalls, Kingston upon Thames. She appeared in a number of movies including *London Town* with comedian Sid Field and, alongside two actors with local (Sutton) connections, Jack Warner and Jimmy Hanley, in *Here come the Huggetts*. During her recording contract with Pye-Nixa, her 'hit parade' included *Memories are made of this* and *The little shoemaker*. In June 1956 she paid a return visit to St Anthony's Hospital to open a fête to raise funds for hospital radio (on the first occasion she was there as a patient).

The Rolling Stones

The Rolling Stones. The first Surrey performance of all five lads was at the Red Lion, Sutton (see *A Century of Sutton*, 2000) early in 1963. The following winter they had two gigs at the Baths Hall, Epsom. When touring in the area, they would hire a room at the Spring Hotel, Ewell and relax between performances. Clockwise from left: Bill Wyman, Brian Jones, Keith Richards, Charlie Watts, Mick Jagger. Their road manager was Ian Stewart, who lived in Banstead.

Cloaked in secrecy, on the morning of 21 January 1966, guitarist, George Harrison was married at Epsom Register Office to model Pattie Boyd; they had appeared together in the pop group's first movie *A Hard Day's Night*. Beatles' manager Brian Epstein was best man, and Paul McCartney was among the guests. The couple later divorced. The death of this much-admired musician was announced as this book went to press.

8
Nearby: Ashtead, Banstead

The Street, Ashtead, looking south-west, *c.* 1910. Part of the old turnpike road from Epsom to Dorking, The Street had taken over from Rectory Lane as the main shopping area by 1900, although it still contained a number of cottages. The north side of The Street was little changed from farming days, with Street Farmhouse and its fenced-in fields as far west as the corner of Woodfield Lane (far right, with the Brewery Inn visible beyond). The inn began as a beer shop in the mid-nineteenth century, with brewing added not long after. It was rebuilt some seventy years ago. For generations the village shops were family-owned, a situation sustained well into the second half of the twentieth century.

The Hut, Ashtead. Captain (later Colonel) A.C. Gleig acquired various properties in Ashtead, including parts of New Purchase Farm where he built a house he named Murreys Court, and six acres of Parson's Meadow, rented by Miss Jessie Elliston in 1901 and which eventually became the core of Parsons Mead school for girls (see p. 118). In about 1875 he was living at The Hut, a humble name for such an imposing residence, off Ottways Lane.

Woodfield House. With the railway station close by, Ashtead Woods was a favourite Sunday School outing location, with Felton's bakery able to cater for large groups of children. Indeed, the message on the reverse of this postcard view, sent to an address in Putney on 27 July 1909, indicates that 'Charlie' was taking part in such an outing at the time. The youngsters could sit down to a bumper tea in the long refreshment hut (to left of telegraph pole), or play on the swings and other fairground attractions (far left).

St George's Church, Barnett Wood Lane, Ashtead. The church was consecrated on 21 April 1906, succeeding the 'iron church' which had served the community to the west of the village since 1882. I was told that this first little building was lifted, placed on rollers and moved to a new site – there to serve as a parish room/Boy Scout headquarters – so that construction work could begin on the new church. As with a number of churches erected at that time (St John the Baptist, Belmont, was another), building was interrupted by the outbreak of the First World War.

The Street, Ashtead, looking north. Framing this postcard view, both village inns, The Brewery (left) and the Leg of Mutton and Cauliflower (right) are on the sites of much older buildings. The Brewery started life as a beer shop, while the Leg in the early nineteenth century was part of a larger complex that included a farm and even served as a temporary jail. With no street lighting, large lanterns like the Brewery's advertised the presence of the inn and aided travellers in the dark.

Parsons Mead School, *c.* 1910. Originally founded by Miss Jessie Elliston (a former governess to many distinguished families) in Ashtead in 1897, expansion necessitated the move to Parsons Mead, Ottoways Lane, in 1904. The modern school caters for some 350 pupils, with latest facilities including science laboratories and a sports hall.

Ashtead Cricket Club. In 1889, city banker Pantia Ralli acquired Ashtead Park where the cricket club had its pitch. On 4 May 1956, celebrating their seventieth anniversary with a dinner at the Memorial Hall, club members had as one of their distinguished guests eighty-four-year-old Charles Burgess Fry ('CB'), the well-known and highly popular writer and speaker on cricket and other sports. He was presented with the club tie and made an honorary member of the ACC. *

The parish church of St Giles, Ashtead. The church, mentioned by Samuel Pepys in his diary for 1663, stands near the site of an Iron Age stockade and a Roman villa. It has undergone many alterations since the first stone building, dated to about 1125. One of its greatest treasures is the three-light window above the altar, said to have been made well over four hundred years ago by Lombard of Liège. Soldiers from both world wars who worshipped here are remembered by regimental colours and gifts of church furniture.

Sir Lewis Casson and Dame Sybil Thorndike on stage, 1949. During the Second World War, when their elder son John, a Fleet Air Arm pilot, was a prisoner of war, his wife Patricia and their three children, together with his sister Ann, jointly acquired Thirty Trees, a house in Ashtead. Worshippers of that time later told me that Dame Sybil was often to be seen at early morning service at the parish church, having come directly from wherever in London's theatreland she was appearing. John was repatriated in 1945 and on VE day reached Thirty Trees, where there were soon ecstatic reunions.

High Street, Banstead, *c.* 1910. 'The place where beans grow' appeared in Domesday with twenty-eight villagers, fifteen cottagers and seven slaves. The name of the old Woolpack Inn (above, left) is a reminder of another ancient agricultural activity, that of sheep-farming. From the 300 ft deep well at the south edge of the Downs, the main street led past the inn, and the smithy opposite the parish church (see p. 121). The lower view, looking north, was I believe photographed from the church tower. Somewhere on land to the left of the horse-drawn carriage was the old pond, drained in 1929.

Nork Park, 1905. The former estate of Mr Colman, the 'mustard millionaire', lay between the Downs and Banstead, near Tattenham Way, with many acres of farm and parkland. Nearby Tumble Beacon was once an important link in the chain of high points where fires could be lit as signals of emergency (invasion) or celebration. Great Burgh (see p. 124) was built by Mr Colman for his son's marriage.

All Saints' Church, Banstead. It seems likely that a place of worship has been on this site for more than a thousand years. During their courtship my parents often walked across the Downs from Belmont to attend Evensong here, and regular visits were made all through my childhood to attend to family graves. Favourite texts and wall-paintings had been whitewashed during 'improvements' to the interior, but the west window, designed by Dante Gabriel Rosetti and made at the William Morris works, remained.

The chapel, Garratts Hall. The family associated with this large house at the western end of Banstead village could trace their ancestors back to one Thomas Gerard, the chief landowner, well over five hundred years earlier. The name changed by way of Garrard into Garratt. A girls' school flourished in the house for some time; by the end of the nineteenth century it was in the hands of the Lambert family, for whom my maternal grandmother worked when a young woman. The house was demolished in about 1933.

The Dutch garden, Rose Hill School, Park Road. The school occupied a house dating from 1770, which had been known as Rooks' Nest; Rose Hill was then a nearby farm. A further name change came about in 1966, when the firm of Galliford Seear moved in. They called it Castle House, from the motif of their company badge.

Banstead railway station. The London, Brighton and South Coast Railway extended its London–Sutton line to Epsom Downs via Belmont and Banstead in May 1865. Set in the midst of downland, the station was surprisingly busy, partly because of the number of visitors to hospitals and similar institutions in the neighbourhood, and partly because raceday specials also attracted passengers. For thirty years from 1898 the station was known as Banstead and Burgh Heath; the one-stage single fare to Belmont at about that time was 1½d. In the 1930s 'Southern Railway Banstead Station' was painted in large white letters on the roof, serving as a marker for pilots seeking to land their planes at the increasingly busy Croydon Aerodrome, some nine miles to the north-east.

High Street, Banstead. After the pond was drained, fine parades of shops were developed on the west side of the old street, although older premises opposite remained. Among them, my grandfather's bakery survived for some years; his customers included several boarding schools in the area, and also Banstead Hospital (3rd Middlesex County Lunatic Asylum), built in 1877 to accommodate 2,500 patients. Banstead village school (attended by my mother from 1910 to 1911) was demolished in 1992 and a Waitrose store built on the site.

Great Burgh, Reigate Road, 1948. The back of the house looks across acres of its own land towards the golf course and to the racecourse beyond. Built for Mr Colman jnr (see p. 121), it was little used as a private residence but, with a number of laboratory buildings in the grounds, became the research and development department of the Distillers' Company, and thereafter for other scientific purposes by British Petroleum and Smith, Klein & Beecham.

Nork Parish Church. Civic Sunday, 15 April 1956, saw the new Vicar of Nork, the Revd Leonard Carey conducting his first services in the parish church. He promised to introduce a shortened form of Matins and a family service for Sunday mornings. The procession to the church (above) included Councillor Reginald Bevis, chairman of Banstead Council, with officers and members and their families. *

Banstead British Legion. In the mid-1950s the local branch came up with an idea to ease the parking problem in Banstead High Street by acquiring land behind their premises for a car park to hold two hundred vehicles. Captain A. Wolfe and Colonel D.O. May of British Legion Attendants Limited, who would administer such a scheme, visited the site with Mr L.F. Hoather, the branch chairman. It was intended that local disabled ex-servicemen would be employed to supervise the car park. Above, inspecting the site, left to right are Captain Wolfe, Colonel May and Mr Hoather. * The British Legion hall in High Street, not far from the Victoria public house (named for the carriage, not the queen), was a popular venue for wedding receptions and similar events (right).

Farewell. To quote the great Lord Rosebery's words of long ago: 'Suffice it to say that the name of Epsom remains immortal, and so long as horses and sport exist, must so continue.' For many, Epsom still is horses – their care, their training, their racing, their grace and beauty. So I leave readers with one last reminder of what saved the town when the spa failed, and what continues to bring it to the forefront of our minds on at least one day each year.

BRITAIN IN OLD PHOTOGRAPHS

To order any of these titles please telephone our distributor,
Haynes Publishing, on 01963 442105
For a catalogue of these and our other titles please telephone
Joanne Govier at Sutton Publishing on 01453 732423